OFFBEAT BAJA

This book is dedicated to
Erle Stanley Gardner, a man
who knew, understood, and
without reservation loved
Baja California

Offbeat Baja

by Jim Hunter

with photographs by Robert Western

CHRONICLE BOOKS  SAN FRANCISCO

Photographs on pages 13, 14, 21, 30, 41, 45, 50, 55, 66, 69, 80, 81, 82, 87, 97, 99, 105, 107, 109, 118, 123, 129, 145 and 146 by Robert Western
All others by the author

Library of Congress Cataloging in Publication Data

Hunter, Jim, 1937-
    Offbeat Baja.

      1. Baja California—Description and travel—1951-
—Guide-books. I. Title.
F1246 .H86   917.2'2   77-5738
ISBN 0-87701-093-5

Chronicle Books
870 Market Street
San Francisco
California 94102

CONTENTS

ACKNOWLEDGEMENTS

No guidebook reaches print without help from a great number of people. The kind and quantity of help may differ, but all of it is important. Certain among their number deserve special thanks: Richard Carroll, for his support and encouragement; José Alfaro Salés, of the Mexican Department of Tourism, for his enthusiastic support throughout; Robert Western, for being not only an expert professional photographer but also a fearless companion; those many Honda dealers up and down California and Arizona, and particularly Dave Peterson and John Bridges, and the shop staff at Salinas Honda who gave invaluable assistance and technical advice. In Baja, Antero Diaz, of Bahia de Los Angeles; the staff and management of Exportadora de Sal in Guerrero Negro; Mr. & Mrs. Francisco Muñoz, of Guerrero Negro; that extraordinary human being in San Ignacio, Padre Jaime Francez; Reuben Brooks, in Santa Rosalia; Aurelio Robinson, in Loreto; Carlos Garciglia, in Guerrero Negro, who, among his many other abilities, can recite from memory Garcia Lorca's poetry; in La Paz, Francisco Arámburo S.; and, for their repeated and warm hospitality, Miguel Macias and Al Sanchez; the men and women of the lonely ranchos who were unfailing in their good humor and willingness to give a lost gringo directions and help. And there are those special few to whom no thanks are ever adequate. They are the Yett family of Escondido: Ron, Bonny, Brett, and Deedee, who launched with unflagging interest and loving support each Baja trip; and my daughter Sarah and my wife Mary, who had to wave, when they were not going to Baja with me, all those hard good-byes. God bless each of you.

INTRODUCTION

This book is about dirt-Baja: the long, mountainous peninsula rich with the forgotten and the hard to reach; the special, the hidden, and the often overlooked.

There is the Baja California that we know little of. It's reaching *that Baja* this book is concerned with. The new paved road, dedicated in 1973, is opening doorways to exploration from one end of Baja clear to the other. Of course it is true that most of the old Baja-1000 road is gone forever. But that old road wasn't the only road in Baja. And the stops along it weren't the only sights to see. Far from it.

A new generation of "Baja Hands" is finding different bays, new beaches, and remote mountain villages. They are rediscovering places by-passed by the new road. And the accounts they return with tell of long, untouched coastlines, and of a huge, largely unknown interior.

The *Baja-Dirt-Road-Classification-System* at the beginning of this book, and the many road-logs inside it, describe in detail what to expect of Baja's backroads. The road-logs and RCS make it possible, for the first time, to establish comparative degrees of Baja driving difficulty.

Half the research for this book was accomplished traveling in a 1970 Toyota FJ-55 4WD Land-Cruiser Wagon, the rest over many years on various motorcycles (both street and dirt), bus, hitchhiking, plane, and motorhoming.

Distances were checked, sometimes double-checked, with accurate odometers and trip-gauges. But accuracy will vary with tire and rim size, and with the condition of the indicator, so it's worth spending $10 to get your odometer checked before entering the parts of Baja where its accuracy is all-important.

I suppose any traveler has a desire to share joyful discoveries with others. And this book is an extension of beach and cross-road questions I first began answering in the early '70s when I was walking in Baja.

Not every Baja back road is in this book. Nor is there, for instance, a full discussion of Baja's most interesting offroad treasure: its mysterious and multiple cave paintings. That's because only one such site is accessible without a mule and a guide, and because Harry Crosby's fine book on the paintings is available. However, the more than 50 offbeat roads and destinations included here, and the surprises that go with them, are among Baja's best.

Baja is a rough frontier of cowboys and ranchos. At the same time it is a boiling agricultural and urban phenomenon. For its small population of about 2 million people is not only busy in the mountains and on the sea coasts, but is also reclaiming the deserts and building new cities.

And while the long, active peninsula remains surrounded by blue seas it is starved for water. What vegetation and animal life persist there survive on sea mists, mountain springs and snows, rare rains, and supplies of water trapped underground centuries before. On the long Magdalena Plain big government pumping projects tap these subterranean reserves to turn the desert surface green with crops. And Ciudad Constitucion, once the tiny village of El Crucero, is moving rapidly toward a population of 50,000 people.

Off the beaten track, the remote, the unusual and the untouched are realistic goals.

The place we call Baja is actually two Mexican states: Baja California (given statehood in 1952) and Baja California Sur (1974). It is both an economic and geographic frontier; trade restrictions are relaxed and opportunities greater than on mainland Mexico. Proximity to Alta California, the little brother now a giant member of the United States, also has a strong influence on Baja California.

It is a strange and wild place, and because of the new blacktop the old standbys are easier to reach and for the first time the remote, the unusual, and the untouched are realistic goals.

BEYOND THE BLACKTOP

Answers about Baja beyond the blacktop are here. But no journey into Baja is either all off the road or all on the road. The proportions of each vary according to supplies of gasoline and food and according to individual preference. The four-wheeler and biker are often on the blacktop and the motorhome driver is sometimes in the dirt.

A crucial fact for anyone going off the blacktop is important: *Off the carretera the jump from the comfort and safety of highway to the discomfort and danger of tough back road is immediate.* Grading is rare, bridges few, ruts and rocks and high crowns are common. Devilish and seemingly unending washboards are rampant, and grueling climbs in and out of dry arroyos over large rocks and loose sand a regular ingredient in the Baja offroad driving diet.

The new country being opened up is as tough as the old—perhaps tougher. The old dirt road was once the main road.

The new tourist in dirt-Baja today has a rare chance to be early in reaching the previously inaccessible, to view unique areas, to interact with Mexican pioneers who seem in some ways to have stepped out of the history of the American west—and to do this without having first to invest in a 1000 miles of tough, dangerous dirt driving.

A seldom traveled road in Baja.

A FEW URGENT WORDS

Basic life-and-death rules about Baja ought to be given here. Although no one can tell anyone else exactly what to take or how to prepare, some requirements are universal, and no one leaving the blacktop should ignore them.

They are: personal preparation by each member of a party by careful reading of several sources; questioning of experienced persons and local residents who understand the goal and the country; rudimentary knowledge of the vehicle used and some ability to make the inevitable minor repairs; *proper tools* (not just a factory-supplied tool kit) a ratchet set specifically for your equipment and other top quality tools; water, first-aid items, head coverings.

And finally, no experienced person enters into any challenge with the desert, or the desert mountains or beaches, or any wilderness, without first informing someone as to where he will go and when he may be expected to return.

Maps: Some maps of Baja are not accurate; the best are unable to keep up with the swiftly changing roads. Where a map indicates one road you may find three. And where you expect to drive confidently to an intersection marked 20 miles away, five intersections not indicated on the map will appear on the way. Which is the right one?

Your best friend on the back roads is a trustworthy odometer or the more easily used trip-gauge. Even better is someone who's been there before. Signs are largely unknown. In Baja the assumption is that if you are there *you know* where you are going.

Mapping and traveling Baja's back roads is a still-emerging, changing science. That may explain in part the attraction that these half-forgotten, tough old roads hold for so many people. Out in the mountains or at desert crossroads, books and maps, however valuable their help, will never give all the answers you want. *Judgment and luck* are still a big part of Baja travel and maybe it's that spice and tingle of worry that keeps pulling gringo adventurers back.

THE MEXICAN DRIVER

The Mexican driver will tax you considerably, but he is neither superior nor inferior to his American counterpart—he is just different. Driving courtesy in Mexico is not contagious, but rather is considered a form of mental retardation peculiar to Americans.

The horn, fist-shaking, the evil glare, the epithet, and the auto itself are all readily used tools of the Mexican driver. The horn, which is the most often used, means: I am coming. I am not halting. If you want to continue living, get rapidly out of my way!

Pedestrians have few rights. Mexican drivers expect certain automatic behavior from their intimidated walkers. If you intend to move about Baja on foot, learn what that expected behavior is and practice it. The primary rule is: The pedestrian is always wrong, the auto always right.

THE MEXICAN DREAM

It does not exist.

Only last year two young men swung happily into a north La Paz filling station, their blue eyes gleaming, their blond hair waving. They called out loudly to me, "Hey man! Where's all the señoritas?"

There are none. They always have been, and still are, for the señors only. Change is taking place, but nothing so swift as to alter that basic cultural fact.

Other Americans race to Mexico for the lower cost of living, and with the September 1976 devaluation of the peso, which altered the long-standing exchange rate from 12½ pesos to 20 pesos for one dollar, prices will be lower, for Americans—but probably only for a while.

Prices are high in Baja. Gasoline and supplies may now cost slightly less than in the States. At the old exchange rate they were more—gas, for instance, was 85¢ a gallon. And we can expect prices to continue to rise in Baja.

The Mexican dream you acquire is what will pull you back again and again to Baja. And this happens usually after direct contact with the people not as a tourist but as a human being.

The residents, or "Californianos," are proud to be a part of Mexico's frontier. They have a sense of being involved in something important and historic, much like Americans in Alaska, and they know they are different from the rest of Mexico, yet inextricably a vital part of it. The surges of hope, excitement, and opportunity which are present in Baja are not duplicated on the mainland.

The Mexican government is mildly irritated by the use of the word Baja as an improper reference to the two separate states, but it seems as if the word is here to stay. Americans have invested it with a holy combination of mystery, adventure, bad roads, competition, ocean and beaches. And though literally it means only "lower," its emotional connotations are practically endless.

Don't get hung up in Baja on the words "inferior"

and "superior." They don't fit. The word that does is "different." In both customs and language the people of Baja are far more conservative than their fellow North Americans, the yankees.

In a La Paz cantina in 1974 a 40-year-old Mexican electrician embraced me and tried to sum up how he felt about yankees. He said it slowly so I was sure to understand his Spanish: "My friend," he leaned back with outspread arms, smiling. "Mexico and the United States—they are like two bothers in the same house. And someday," he winked, "they will understand and love each other."

ONWARD

Baja California is a clean place. The various bacteria present probably affect the American digestive system less than the careless use of Mexican hot-sauce and tequila chasers. Sure, I love *la salsa*, too, and there is usually a moment requiring tequila, but when I don't use them I don't get sick.

Some people think Baja looks dirty. Take a close look at your own city back home and see if the paint on city hall or the federal building isn't peeling, or if the sidewalks aren't unswept or sinking. Americans have an amazing facility for finding fault with anything Mexican while remaining blind to identical shortcomings in their own country.

As you move about in Baja give the people you meet there the respect and courtesy their own lives, works, goals, and dreams demand and deserve.

Remember you are on vacation and they are working. And to their ears your language is outlandish and churlish. Don't lapse into impatience. Patience and humility will go a long way toward transporting *you* to *your* Mexican dream.

One dream that does come true in Baja California, is that of an unspoiled wilderness populated by a strong and generous people. And I do not write without the nagging fear that additional tourism will impair that condition.

My hope is that Baja California will make of its visitors lasting friends: friends who will care strongly about what they have seen in the land and in the people, and treat each with respect; friends who, through their knowledge, love, and understanding of this wild place, will be ready to use it and alert to protect it.

Jim Hunter

Monterey, California.
February 1977.

ROAD-LOG & CLASSIFICATION SYSTEM

Each person exploring Baja must exercise his own judgment. The following road-log and dirt-road classifications are tools to assist the process. Whether or not a route will be negotiable will often depend on a person's driving skill rather than road surface or equipment used. And some roads in Baja that appear on maps as black lines are much different from others so identified.

One afternoon I met a man in a two-wheel drive half-ton pickup hauling a 10-foot cab-over-camper confidently toward La Purisima. He was just a few miles from the blacktop but he planned to drive to La Purisima and then back to Loreto for dinner!

And then there are roads that are good most of the way but have two or three bad sections that might make the route impossible. The logs and classification system describe these bad sections and offer a driver a chance to weigh them against his particular skills and equipment.

The system doesn't cover every kind of vehicle, so adjustments are necessary. A four-wheel-drive pickup with a big camper is going to fall somewhere between a regular pickup and a four-wheel-drive vehicle with no camper. The same is true of motorcycles. A bike on a day-trip will breeze over some bad spots, but a loaded-down bike is going to have real trouble.

Looking at the road-logs the first time someone might ask, "Why all this detail?" or wonder why distances are measured to the tenth of a mile. The answer is that when you are out *there*, you will want badly to know where you are, and one purpose of the road-logs is to let you know where you are as often as possible.

The approach to a Class VI downgrade.

As soon as you pass a fork or turnoff—and the turnoffs are never on any map—your mind will leap with questions: "Am I on the right road? Did I make a wrong turn? Do I have enough gas to wander around out here?" And so in the absence of topographic maps and star-sightings, the road-logs are a system of "cactus-navigation."

They include as many identifiable geographic and manmade structures as possible—even overturned autos—for when you are bouncing around out in the desert wondering where you are, finding the next detail is going to be like finding a gold mine.

A last word on running these roads. They are going to seem more difficult the first few hours than they really are. And this will be because it takes everyone

—four-wheelers, bikers, and truckers—a few days or a few hours *to get their road rhythm* and the feel again of their rig on rocks and dirt. When it comes you will know it, and the pleasure of being in graceful control of a fine machine will make the roads less disagreeable than otherwise. A final warning on weight is necessary, particularly to bikers: If you are overweight you will never get your road rhythm and your trip will never be enjoyable.

Baja Dirt Road Classifications I to X

Class   Description

I.   *Family auto recommended:* two-lane, 20 foot wide, graded, treated dirt surface; few holes, ruts, or eroded portions.

II.   *Family auto possible:* one-lane, 10-foot wide, occasionally graded, untreated dirt surface with holes, bumps, and minor erosion. No steep grades, no difficult arroyo crossings, small motorhomes using great care may negotiate.

III.   *Pickup truck recommended:* one-lane, 8 to 10-feet wide; extremely rare grading; ruts increase in depth; numerous holes, rocks, bumps, and increasing erosion. Grades increase but present no hazards. Vans and pickups with *small* campers may expect to complete without great risk or great difficulty, but motorhomes should never attempt.

IV.   *Pickup truck possible:* narrow one-lane; high-clearance essential; never graded or treated; holes, rocks, and bumps increase in number and size. Spots of serious erosion. Grades increase and present hazards. At the bottom and top of grades the spinning tires of two-wheel-drive vehicles have created deep waves in the road surface.

Vans and pickups with campers can negotiate only with difficulty and the risk of damage. Family autos should never attempt.

V.   *Pickup truck possible with great care:* narrow lane with holes, rocks, and bumps. Arroyo crossings required. Grades will not exceed 20°. Sand and high crowns make two-wheel traction difficult. Waves increase in size. Vans and pickups with campers should never attempt.

VI.   *Four-wheel-drive recommended:* narrow lane; holes, rocks, and bumps continuous; arroyo crossings and arroyo travel common. Grades will have loose rocks, gravel and deep waves but will not exceed 30°. Steep cliffs, and often deep dust will occur. *Motorcycles and dune buggies will get their first challenge and difficulty.* Two-wheel-drive pickups will negotiate only with difficulty and the risk of damage.

VII.   *Four-wheel-drive required:* narrow lane; large rocks imbedded in road; no shoulders, cactus close-by on both sides of road; long stretches with no pullouts; stream bed work required more than half the time; multiple washouts; work with a shovel not uncommon. Grades will not exceed 35° but waves at top and bottom, if hit too fast, will damage rig. Two-wheel-drive pickup trucks may attempt but damage will occur.

VIII.   *Four-wheel-drive essential:* narrow lane; constant hazards in road; road may occasionally disappear into cactus and riverbed or the loose rocky plain of a mesa or ridge top. Path will be difficult to follow. This class may be either a road with very little use or one with steep grades and/or poor surface. *Motorcycles must use great caution to avoid accidents, particularly downhill.* The challenge to dune buggies is moderate. Grades will not exceed 40°. Two-wheel-drive pickup trucks should never attempt.

IX. *Four-wheel-drive possible with great care:* alternating lane and absence of track; constant danger from large rocks; holes in road; waving of surface; and in other terrain deep ruts, unstable surface, and cactus spines. Repairs and delays may be expected. Work with a shovel common. Begin to encounter wandering cattle and goats and horsemen. There is a disturbing absence of motor-vehicle tracks while those of cattle and other animals predominate. Motorcycles will complete this class only at great risk. With experienced drivers dune buggies may go in and out without damage. Two-wheel-drive pickup trucks cannot expect to return. Grades may exceed 45°.

X. *All motorized vehicles should avoid:* trail with broken stretches of two paths. There are very few stretches of this class within roads. Most Class X occurs at the end of other roads. They go nowhere and are dangerous because of the chance of getting lost. No one uses them, and breakdown and damage are likely.

1

THE PACIFIC SIDE

"I don't know why you want to go there.
On the Pacific the wind blows all the time.
The water is always cold.
There are no facilities—nothing."

Mexican Government official, 1976

"In the late afternoon light . . . the landscape
was like a fairyland . . . ."

Eliot Porter,
Baja California and the Geography of Hope, 1967.

"Here urbanization ends as though
it had been chopped off with a knife."

Erle Stanley Gardner,
The Hidden Heart of Baja, 1962.

"Baja, in large part, is one of the most arid
and forbidding landscapes on earth."

William Weber Johnson,
Baja California, 1972

"Now and then in the dull records of a whaling
station there is an entry . . . a whale with primitive,
half-formed *hind-legs* protruding from its body is
brought to the whaling deck."

Victor B. Scheffer,
The Year of The Whale, 1969.

THE DISTANT PACIFIC

Santa Catarina Desembarcadero: An early test of
how seriously you want to explore Baja is the old haul
road into Catarina Landing. After traveling it you
will have answers to many questions about Baja's
offbeat roads, and the chances are good that the balance of Baja will beckon.

Depending on how often you halt to rest, take
pictures, and check road conditions, it takes four to
six hours to travel the 40-mile distance from blacktop
to Catarina on the Pacific Ocean. The desert scenery
on the way, the beach and ocean once you have
arrived, and the solitude of this once-busy shipping
point make a journey into Catarina worth the effort.

Once at the end of this road, as with many in Baja,
the sky and the desert beach are your roof and room,
and the stars and wind your companions for the stay.
And though the Pacific enjoys a reputation for fog
and wind, I have found this long stretch of deserted
Pacific Coast to be sunny and generally wind free in
the winter months.

There is desert wildlife along the Catarina road,
where I have seen both fox and coyote. Keep alert,

*San Cristobal beach 14 miles north of Cabo San Lucas on a
little known dirt road, looking north toward El Migriño.*

too, for the half-wild burros and mules as well as the inevitable underfed desert cattle always near the tiny Mexican ranchos that dot Baja from top to bottom.

The turnoff to Catarina, 38 miles south of El Rosario, is always difficult to find. It is exactly 3.7 miles south of the old cafe and windmill at El Progreso, and 1.7 miles south of the cafe with the road sign announcing *Cecelia Station.* Approached from the south it is 11.3 miles north of the government parador and Pemex station at San Agustin.

For those traveling south the turn is to the right (west), and fishermen will occasionally erect a weatherworn wooden sign, facing north only, that reads:

> *Rancho Station Catarina   35 km*
> *Gasolina, Puerto Catarina 63 km*

However, gasoline is no longer sold at the rancho on the way—nor is it sold at El Progreso or Cecelia Station. El Rosario or San Agustin Parador are the two choices for filling up before running in.

And it can indeed be a long run in, because this innocent-looking turnoff, with a light wind whipping up the sand near the blacktop, is the gateway to over 200 miles of desolate coastal roads and mountain cutoffs, and cliffs and beaches similar to those along California's southern coast.

Between October and March a few scattered tiny groups of lobster fishermen do inhabit some of the beaches reached by the Catarina turnoff. During the rest of the year an occasional fisherman will battle his way from the interior of Baja to harvest fish. These fishermen may sell you gasoline from their 55-gallon drums. And then again they may not, so do not depend on them for gasoline.

Except for their supplies there is no water, gasoline, food, or any services whatsoever, either at Catarina Landing or for the 200 miles of deserted coast to the south, should you desire, after practicing on Catarina, to challenge it. You must carry everything you require.

Logs and a description of the balance of the coast follow after the Catarina Road-Log. Mile 0 is at the right-hand turnoff from Mex 1. From there the gravel road winds into rocky cactus-covered hills, drops into

From October to March this lonely beach at Santa Catarina Landing is occupied by a small group of lobster fishermen.

a tiny valley, passes Rancho Catarina, tops a startling plateau with views in all directions and elephant, yucca, and boojum trees in abundance, as well as cardon and columnar cactus mixed in with the prominent spindly armed, red-flowered ocotillos. Expect to encounter blossoms of many colors at almost any time in Baja.

From the plateau the road drops sharply and winds 10 miles to the sea. The old landing is now little more than memory. On the kelp-strewn beach of wet, black rocks, the only relic of its history is an assemblage of large orange and white blocks of onyx.

Until the late 1950s thousands of tons of blocks like these were hauled from El Marmol and shipped north from Catarina to satisfy a worldwide demand for onyx pen-and-pencil desk sets.

At Catarina the beach is long and wide and generally free of rocks. Gathering a half-bucket of clams is a 30-minute task, but it's best to begin several hundred yards south of the fishing camp. Behind the beach the gray and white sands roll back into a wide, alluvial plain dotted with green brush and cactus.

On either side of the plain stand high mesas, between which the road enters. The water is too cold for swimming and too rough for diving, but the surf, when the wind dies, brings in a long wave. When the

The bridge at 34.3 mile is still in use and many a heavily loaded onyx truck has passed over it.

lobster fishermen are there they dive in the early morning in wet suits.

It would take a long time just to explore this one Pacific beach. On the high cliff behind the fishing camp is a small cemetery and on the north and south ends of the long beach are tidal pools and cliffs.

In season the fishermen's huts fly red and green flags to help the divers relocate camp. By noon the wooden boats are pulled far back up on the slippery rocks.

A few years back I met three young boys working Catarina alone. Their routine, they said, was six weeks on and two weeks off during the 6-month season. The boys belonged to a cooperative located just south of Ensenada. The lobster they caught were kept fresh in cages lowered into the ocean, and when enough had accumulated they were hauled out in a two-ton stake-bed truck whose drivers regularly negotiated the tough 40 miles.

The road is single lane all the way and by Baja standards is in good shape. Four-wheel-drive is not essential, but a good truck is. The worst grade is 29 miles in and several minor challenges exist along the way.

Going to Catarina is a good test of offroad skills, and as with so many other roads in Baja, what kind of vehicle you can get over them depends less on the road itself than on your driving skills. One man's four-wheel-drive road might be another's pickup road, and so on with motorcycles and dune buggies.

The last mile into Catarina, just before the beach, is over hardpacked sand and should present no problems. Overall the road to Catarina is Class III and IV going in, and the grade at 28.9 miles is Class IV down and Class V coming back up.

MILE CATARINA LANDING & CANOAS TURN

0 Catarina Landing turnoff 3.7 south of El Progreso, 11.3 north of San Augustin Parador. Road leaves blacktop highway west.

.5 Good overnight camping area for large rigs in grassy draw, large turnaround. Proceed through gravel pit on to gently rising plateau, reach ridge top and start down narrow road.

8.5 Jct. with poor road from left. Do not attempt this exit on return though it is shorter if going south. It is poor road.

9.3 Abandoned auto, '41 Dodge serial #588-ITDS. You're on the right road.

12.5 Well, windmill, abandoned buildings, shade trees, wide spot in valley to park and rest, boulder-covered hills, tall cardon cactus.

19.5 Rough section of road, permanent big rocks. Check it first, then climb over it slowly. Short, but be careful with the crankcase.

20.4 Area of Rancho Catarina. Airstrip to left on plateau, drop down into shady area with buildings up low hill to right, corral to left. No gas, no food, no facilities. Chickens, directions, and friendship.

20.7 Begin climb out from rancho after going through center. This stretch of loose, steep road is short but bad. It is 2.2 miles to Canoas turnoff.

The author at Punta Canoas during a three day run down the deserted west coast.

22.6 Jct. with road to Canoas to left, straight ahead for Catarina; pile of rocks marks intersection. Now you will wind 6 miles through low hills moving steadily upward to a high, flat plateau.

28.9 Top plateau for striking view in all directions, sea in distance. Flat stop for resting, limited shade, steep drop down from here. *Without 4WD, you will question if you wish to continue.* It is not a matter of going down but of coming back out, so you may choose to walk a half mile down the road and stretch your legs while looking it over. This is the hardest part of the road to drive.

34.3 Wooden bridge. You will want to first test it on foot.

38.5 Reach the flats after winding 10 miles through low, red, cactus-covered hills. Road, hardpacked limestone and sand, is level.

39.0 Maze of roads to sea, sand dunes and arroyo; pick a route carefully by keeping generally straight and to the right. Major left winds to nearby point .3 miles.

39.8 Road ends at grassy sand dune. Catarina Landing. Three huts. Old blocks of onyx lay on the beach where the sea is reducing them to sand. End.

This Log: Classes III through VI

Punta Canoas from Catarina Landing Road: The abrupt headland seen in the distance south of Catarina is Punta Canoas, the site of a second fishing camp. The valley behind the headland looks more like a moonscape than a part of the Baja coast. But the beach itself is superior to Catarina. It is larger, wider, and provides more shelter. And as with the balance of the Distant Pacific of Baja, the greatest offering at Canoas is open, unpopulated beaches, sea shells and driftwood, an abundance of bird and marine life, and a great feeling of discovery.

The fishing camp here is similar to the one at Catarina but is larger. Consequently there is litter on the beach near the camp. To avoid it, plan on camping in the center or at the southern end of Canoas beach. However, because the fishermen usually enjoy an afternoon or evening visit, you needn't hesitate to approach them. On the other hand, they will respect your privacy. When you do visit them, don't be surprised when you are offered lobster or clams. Lobster dinner on the Distant Pacific is not uncommon, so you will want to be prepared to cook it.

The turnoff for Canoas is 22.6 miles west of the blacktop on the Catarina Road, and the three-hour run in from that point is 25 miles long. The road is not as good as that to Catarina because it gets less use.

Expect Class III and IV to Canoas, with increasingly numerous short stretches of V.

TO PUNTA CANOAS FROM CATARINA LANDING ROAD

MILE

0 Mile 22.6 left turn off Catarina Landing Road.

1.1 Top rise, meadowlike plateau, many forks

rejoining each other, road is proceeding in a SSW direction toward the sea but will not reach the sea for 25 miles.

4.8 Top low rise.

5.2 Cross arroyo.

5.3 Class IV climb out of arroyo .1.

7.5 High plateau, short upgrade ahead.

9.0 Class V up grade .1.

9.1 Class V down grade .1.

9.4 *Important Junction:* straight ahead to abandoned rancho. Hard right to arroyo leading to Canoas and south. Drop into riverbed. Move west.

10.3 Road continues west in riverbed.

13.1 Exit arroyo, road goes south.

14.0 Large cardon on right.

16.8 Move south in powdery dust over rolling plain. Sea to right.

18.0 Abandoned 1935 4-door Studebaker to right.

19.6 White, flat, barren alluvial plain. Airfield on left. Many forks. Keep right for beach and fishing camp.

19.8 Fork to right. Left for points south. Go right for fishing camp and Punta Canoas beach.

25.1 Fishing camp in lee of low cliff at north end Punta Canoas beach. Beach roads south, some wood for campfires, no trees or cactus, sand dunes offer firm driving, usually no more than 10 persons here in the tiny wooden shacks.

Expect Class III and IV to Canoas from Catarina Road, with several short stretches of Class V. This is no place for an auto but a pickup (even carrying light camper) will negotiate with minimum danger and trouble.

Punta Canoas to the Blacktop at Ejido Juarez: Along the more than 100 miles of dirt road between Punta Canoas and Ejido Juarez lies the last of the great uninhabited stretches of Baja coast accessible by road—an unbroken chain of beaches and mountain plateaus rarely seen by any tourist. The road, although properly called coastal, constantly swings in and out to bypass headlands and high mountains.

It takes a minimum of three driving days from Canoas to the blacktop, so figure on camping out twice, and take some time those evenings to leave the campfire unlit and study the stars. You will be impressed by their clarity and by the number of satellites, and you may perhaps be surprised by a UFO moving across the constellations.

Each time you top a rise on this seemingly endless road and see a clear crescent beach ahead beckoning you on, you will get the answer to the question, "What am I doing here?" Where you want to camp is up to you. From among the many mountain and beach camping spots along the way you can choose according to whether you are a rock hound, birdwatcher, or marine-life enthusiast. Chances are you will see no one else. In two trips I have never seen another auto moving along this stretch.

Although many portions of this isolated road ideally require four-wheel-drive, Mexican fishermen negotiate its entire length in pickups and two-ton flat beds. So can you with a shovel and sweat and help from a partner, if you are really proficient with a pickup and don't mind risking your rig.

The road is similar to that from Catarina to Canoas, but with deterioration around Punta Cono and Punta Maria. *Do not* consider the roads on various maps out to the blacktop. The one from San José is a 40-mile hell of rocks and loose rock grades, and the 25-mile run from Punta Blanca is worse from disuse. Your best shot from San José is on out to Ejido Juarez because the road avoids the really high mountains and bad passes.

At about midway in the journey will be found the fishing camp of Arroyo San José. It is located in a beautiful spot, perched at the edge of a wide, deeply

Mile 12.2 Class VI downgrade and bad arroyo crossing near Los Morros south of Punta Canoas.

penetrating lagoon, on a high point of land that over-looks the sea. There you can get directions and advice from the fishermen.

Leaving the camp the road leads inland over a small hump of land and parallels the north side of the lagoon until a shallow crossing point is reached. Soon after, a major intersection marks the beginning of the truly deserted stretches of the coast.

Sea shells and clams are abundant, the fishing is good, and the road seems to wind endlessly to new beaches. The Pacific swell around Punta Cono and Punta Maria sporadically offers a fairly long, three-foot wave. Determined surfers continually explore and pioneer the roads along this coast in search of the long wave uncrowded by other people. But the kind of surf that exists in upper California, such as, for instance, that along Huntington and Malibu beaches, just hasn't yet been located in lower California. Nevertheless, if you're the kind of surfer who will trade a good wave for a lesser wave all to yourself, then Baja might be the place you want to explore.

From Canoas to the blacktop at Ejido Juarez expect stretches of Class III and IV road with several spots of Class V and some of Class VI.

PUNTA CANOAS TO BLACKTOP AT
MILE   EJIDO JUAREZ ON MEX 1

0 At Punta Canoas beach.

.5 Right turn to south is in this area, but its exact location varies year to year. It crosses arroyo and goes inland another .5 mile before going south through low notch in mesa.

4.1 Road proceeds south after passing through notch.

4.6 Cross arroyo, turn inland, proceed toward the sea.

5.5 Below mesa, road again turns south.

6.3 Fork left, keep right, start ridge-hopping.

8.8 View of ocean.

8.9 Class VII up .3.

9.2 Top grade, ocean view.

9.3 Class VI down grade .3 and begin run west to sea.

10.6 Leave riverbed, ocean view.

11.7 Beach view, fork right to beach .2.

12.1 Road parallels beach on rocky mesa.

12.2 Class VI down grade .2.

15.4 Crescent Bay, abandoned fishing camp of Los Morros, road starts inland.

16.9 Fork left to rancho, keep right.

18.0 Fork right, keep right.

19.3 Arroyo Delfino and beach.

19.5 Fork right to beach .2.

22.0 Leave beach up small canyon with 1 mile Class VI.

22.3 Class VII up .2.

23.1 Ridge-running.

26.1 Ocean view from ridge, begin descent to Arroyo San José.

26.9 Drop to Arroyo San José down Class VII .3.

27.1 Fork left, keep right.

29.3 Arroyo San José beach and ocean.

32.9 Arroyo San José fishing camp, lagoon, long beach to south, rocky point.

33.1 Cross low rise and go east up north side of lagoon.

34.2 Road crosses shallow lagoon.

35.2 *Major Intersection:* road straight ahead goes 40 miles to Cataviña. Loose rocks, 6 to 8 hours required, steep grades, 4WD required on Class VIII sections. Road to right continues south down coast. To the right, abandoned '57 Chevy. At intersections watch for bottles that may contain maps and messages. Please return the contents after examination. Taking right turn road continues as follows:

39.0 Fork right to beach 1 mile. Keep left.

39.8 Parallel beach.

40.7 Leave beach inland.

41.8 Beach to right.

42.6 Crescent beach comes into view, road leaves beach.

43.2 Fork left to rancho, keep right.

45.3 Top high ridge, ocean view.

45.6 Class VIII down grade .5.

46.9 Crescent bay in view.

47.2 Enter large valley.

48.0 Enter plain adjacent to sea, sand dunes to right.

51.1 Enter dry salt flats.

52.1 Beach to right, sand dunes.

52.8 Intersection. Go left. Right ends on point over sea.

55.0 Intersection. Go left or right. Left goes around ridge top down gully. Right goes straight down ridge and along edge of large nearby lagoon.

56.2 Parallel shore of large lagoon 2 miles long and .2 mile wide.

58.4 Fork right to beach .2.

58.7 Red beach cliffs, beach.

60.2 Fork right to beach .2, sand dunes.

60.7 Fork right to beach .2.

61.2 *Major Intersection:* Left fork goes to Las Palomas. Straight goes through a broad, flat, green valley and then up into the hills and over the top to Punta Cono and Punta Maria, joining the left fork in that area. The left fork is better but is also longer and passes through deep dust. If you have 4WD take the right fork. If you don't, take the left. Taking right fork path is as follows:

62.0 Class VII up .7 and begin up onto high ridges.

62.5 Class VII down .5.

62.7 Ocean view.

63.5 Drop down to parallel beach and sand dunes.

66.8 Road leaves beach area and goes inland.

69.8 *Major Intersection:* Four-way. Right to Salinito, straight ahead to continue south, left to Las Palomas road.

70.0 *Major Intersection:* T intersection. Road right continues south, left to Las Palomas Road. There is a cement survey marker here.

70.9 Top ridge.

75.9 Abandoned '56 Chevy Carry-All on top of ridge.

77.2 Class VII down grade .4 and fork right to beach.

78.0 Fork right to beach .7.

80.3 Fork right to beach .2 and lagoon behind.

80.9 Fork right to beach and Punta Cono.

84.4 Leaving area of Punta Cono, crescent beach and sand dunes to right.

84.8 On hillside to left white sea shells arranged to form political sign. Gathering of huts at site of abandoned Ejido.

88.0 Fork right to beach fishing camp .2.

89.2 Fork right to beach.

92.9 Fork right to beach.

93.7 Enter valley with heavy vegetation.

94.1 Class VI upgrade .5.

95.2 Abandoned '61 Chevy Nova overturned.

95.7 Fork right to beach.

96.2 Fork right to beach. Here the road begins to leave the beach areas and angle inland toward the blacktop.

100.7 Ranch road left, keep straight.

104.0 Beach road right, keep straight.

104.6 Beach road right, keep straight.

108.6 Beach road right, keep straight.

109.6 Go east up low hill, canyon to left.

110.3 Enter narrow canyon, large body of alkaline water to left.

112.1 Climb out of canyon to right and descend to wide plain.

113.9 Abandoned rancho to right. Road changes to Class I and II.

115.7 Rancho to right.

117.7 Fork right, keep right.

119.6 Rancho of Ejido Juarez, corral, old cars, blacktop on other side of rancho. End of run. Nearest gas Punta Prieta 7 miles north, or Rosarito 18 miles south.

Expect Classes III and IV on this run with short stretches of V, VI, VII. The problem on this run is not road condition but remaining on the right road.

Malarrimo: Say the name and the heart skips a beat and imagination takes over. Visions of old galleons, bottles with messages from lost mariners, and thoughts of flotsam and jetsam from the entire Pacific flood the mind.

At Malarrimo the landmass of Baja juts out like a giant scoop to catch drift deposited by the Japanese Current. A new route to Malarrimo Beach now makes the journey far shorter than it had been.

But before you rush to Malarrimo, remember you won't be the first to arrive; its deposits have been picked over pretty thoroughly. To avoid disappointment, keep in mind, too, that the currents are not discriminating in what they toss up on Malarrimo Beach. Everything that leaves ships at sea and shores in storm finds its way there, including items you won't be pleased to see, such as plastics and bottles and a seemingly endless supply of light bulbs.

However, there are other objects worth beachcombing for and there are parts of wrecks and old deposits from years past. The Japanese floats though, are all but nonexistent. Sea shells, too, are in shorter supply than on other isolated beaches in Baja.

The beach is typical of those on the Pacific with a short, hard-hitting wave, and generally firm hard-packed black and brown sand backed by low dunes and brown earth. The wind is constant but the arroyo offers shelter for camping.

For those with an appreciative eye, the canyon views on the way in are probably worth more than anything you might find by combing the beach, and spending the starry nights on the Vizcaino Peninsula listening to the coyotes nearby is a reward if the beach is not.

The new, shorter route from Guerrero Negro is 115 miles and 8 hours one-way, a full day each way —and that leaves no time for beachcombing. So Malarrimo is still a three-day affair if you are going to do it right.

Also, you need permission from Expatadora de Sal, the salt company that built the new road over the dikes that places Malarrimo only one day from Guerrero Negro. As long as not too many people ask permission, this easy-going, helpful company is likely to continue to allow occasional tourists to use its road.

Once granted permission at the office in Guerrero Negro, you pass through a guarded gate onto the dike roads and begin meeting the red, two-storey-high salt trucks. The road winds along many dikes, but the proper route follows the main, most-traveled road. This can sometimes be trying since the dikes go on for 30 miles before reaching a big pump station called Bomba Ocho (Pump Eight). Here the road skips across high dunes and, south of Rancho San José de Castro, picks up the old road to Malarrimo.

Stories about the road to Malarrimo paint too bleak a picture. The road from Guerrero Negro to Rancho San José de Castro can be run in a passenger auto, although I wouldn't do it in one I owned. The first 30 miles out of Guerrero Negro to Bomba Ocho are Class I with short stretches of Class II. From the pump to the Rancho it is Class II and III. It is beyond the rancho that the road becomes bad.

From San José de Castro to Malarrimo Beach, a distance of 27 miles, the road generally runs in dry riverbeds; when not in these, it is threading along ridge tops. It is Class IV and V with occasional drops and climbs of Class VI and one Class VII spot. A pickup will get through but a car will not, and a four-wheel-drive would simplify the journey.

There is a good deal of fear about the last two miles down the winding arroyo road to Malarrimo Beach. Blowing sand indeed makes a serious effort to cover the dim track, but conditions are not as bad as usually described.

For instance, late in 1976 a storm blew away the last half-mile of road and pushed the lagoon back up the old arroyo, but the lagoon has since retreated and the road has been pushed back to the beach. If condi-

Near Malarrimo Beach on the Vizcaino Peninsula.

tions are bad at the time of your arrival, camp where you lose the road and walk to the beach.

GUERRERO NEGRO TO MALARRIMO BEACH VIA BOMBA OCHO

MILE

0 At plant office in Guerrero Negro. Pass through gate and when road is not congested speeds up to 40 miles per hour are permissible on this Class I road. *Watch the sharp turns on the ends of some dikes.* Be prepared to see a startling array of shore birds: egrets, herons, godwins, skimmers, pelicans, gulls and many others in this lagoon habitat.

30.0 Bomba Ocho, Pump Eight. A series of red diesel engines pumping seawater into a lagoon for future harvesting of salt. Cross this short pump station, go left at intersection there and proceed south away from the direction you want to go, along the lagoon formed by the pumping action. The road will eventually turn right and go inland toward the road to Malarrimo.

35.6 Road along lagoon turns inland, to the right. Drops to broad plain.

43.3 *Major Intersection:* Road left goes nowhere, ends in deep sand a few miles distant. Road right goes to San José de Castro and you may use it. Road straight ahead also goes to San José de Castro, but is an alternate route. It also goes to Vizcaino back on the blacktop. The turn for Vizcaino is just four miles ahead. If you are going to Malarrimo you should turn right here because this road is easier to follow. The other road is slightly better but has many confusing turnoffs.

49.3 Alternate road comes in from left. You have been traveling straight west across a wide plain toward mountains on the horizon. If you went straight at 43.3 you will come in at this point.

57.3 Fork left to Bahia Asuncion. Sometimes there are red arrows pointing to "B.A." and so keep right here for Malarrimo.

67.6 Enter arroyo and begin south back into mountains after having skirted their northern edge.

71.6 Series of short up-and-down grades.

76.0 Mangesium deposits and old mine site.

82.0 Fork left for Bahia Asuncion. Keep right.

86.4 Rancho San José de Castro is behind a low hill, beside a large pond of spring water, a few small trees, and a fenced corral. Drive into rancho to ask directions for Malarrimo. The road to Malarrimo is around the far side of the pond and is hard to see.

91.4 You have driven away from the rancho and dropped into a little arroyo. There is a fork right. Keep left. Sometimes there is a sign to guide you to Malarrimo.

91.7 Fork right. Go right for Malarrimo. Sometimes there is a sign. You can go beyond this point without 4WD, but I would recommend you did not.

99.5 You are on top of a broad, flat mesa, looking down into a deep canyon. The road runs over big reddish-brown rocks on top the mesa. You have run 8 miles of winding arroyo and then climbed out of it to reach this point. About 2 miles ahead you will descend from this mesa into a wide arroyo that will lead you to Malarrimo. In descending, you will pass through a narrow twisting corkscrew slot.

101.5 Through the slot.

104.5 Enter the arroyo and follow its winding course all the way to the beach. Some sand now begins to fill the road tracks.

108.5 Sand is now plentiful in the arroyo but is generally firm.

112.6 Lagoon appears ahead and road appears to end. Careful use of 4WD will lead the last .5 mile to the beach.

113.1 Malarrimo Beach. It stretches several miles in both directions. Plenty of drift for fires, some sheltered camping spots, low cliffs flank arroyo where it enters sea. Beach is firm enough to support 4WD but has many hidden soft spots. Unless you value what you might find more than your rig, I would recommend you not drive on the beach. Before doing any beachcombing in Baja, make yourself familiar with the federal regulations applicable to finding and removing items from Mexican beaches. Though the laws are not usually enforced, the removal of anything from certain beaches, Malarrimo among them, is technically prohibited.

Expect Class I and II to Bomba Ocho and Class II and III to San José.

Expect Class IV, V, and VI from San José de Castro to Malarrimo.

GUERRERO NEGRO

Guerrero Negro: For centuries whales have been migrating to Scammon's Lagoon, adjacent to Guerrero Negro in Baja California, to calve. Today they continue that migration, but they now share the vast, clear salt-flat lagoons with Expatadora de Sal, a Japanese–Mexican company from which Japan purchases almost its entire national supply of salt. And from commerce in salt has come the dreary company town of Guerrero Negro, which breaks the monotonous flat gray landscape.

Guerrero Negro is there for one reason but tourists enter it for another. The mystery and beauty of the whales attract many pilgrims each spring to the simple town, but most of the tourists depart mildly disappointed: The whales, there from March to June, are not easy to see. To venture out onto the waters for a closer view requires a special expedition, and the lagoon's status as a National Park prohibits indiscriminate interference with the whales.

The old whale-watching spots at the end of company wharves adjacent to the town are closed from time to time. The designated watching point is 20 miles south of Guerrero Negro over dirt roads. The southern entry is marked by small signs depicting blue whales, but the drive in is fairly complicated. And the view of the whales, even with binoculars, is much less spectacular than views of the same groups migrating along the Pacific Coast of the United States.

At the entry to the National Park an old man in a small hut will demand 10 pesos and provide you with a small ticket. A sign nearby declares the intention of the Mexican government to protect the whales.

On the way out it is easy to take a wrong turn, so mark well the route in. If you don't, you will end up out on the salt-flat dikes competing with big trucks for a single lane, with water lapping insistently at your flimsy tires from both sides.

Above all in Guerrero Negro do not attempt to walk anywhere to see anything. Take a taxi or your own auto. The town is in two places, which adds to

At the 28th parallel, the border between Baja California and Baja California Sur, this 140 foot high steel eagle rises abruptly from the flat plains.

the general confusion. The first part of town, consisting of a few motels, service stations, and restaurants, is entered on Mex 1. The second part is past the airport, adjacent to the salt plant and workers' housing. This second area is the main part of Guerrero Negro.

Guerrero Negro, a large town of 5000 people, can look really good when supplies and services are needed. There are many stores, motels, heavy-duty repair shops, a theater, and an airport.

Just north of the town is the large steel eagle com-

The Sarafan Sand Dunes near Guerrero Negro are the exception in Baja and offer a startling departure from other Baja California terrain.

memorating the statehood, in 1974, of Baja California Sur and marking the boundary between the two Bajas. A few miles north of the eagle, which is receiving mixed reactions, lie the mysterious and beautiful white sands of the moving, rolling Sarafan Sand Dunes.

They are pushed inland over green tidelands by the wind, but are not visible from the highway. They are smaller in area but far more dramatic in color than the Oregon Dunes, since they lack any vegetation at all. Named for an old Mexican-Arab who shot geese on the small inlet, the dunes are guaranteed to awe, surprise, please, and, from the high tops of those nearest, to overwhelm with their grandeur and size.

In an area dominated by gray, barren desert constant wind and fog, scudding gray clouds, and an uninteresting, inactive beach, the dunes are an unexpected gift.

Gasoline is the same price as elsewhere in Baja: 4 pesos per litro which works out to 76¢ per gallon. A room for a single person is 70 pesos or $3.50. Hot water is usual, except at the El Presidente. And though perhaps Baja's least attractive town, Black Warrior (Guerrero Negro) remains a friendly place, both at the plant and in the city. And the whales, even if only distantly viewable, are indeed there!

MILE   **WHALE ROAD**

0   Pemex station on Mex 1 on the north portion of Guerrero Negro. From here proceed east out of town to the big Y and from there south toward El Arco on Mex 1.

5.3   Right turn into gravel road off Mex 1 marked by picture of blue whale.

5.6   Right turn off gravel road onto graded dirt road marked by whale. From this point on watch arrows and signs closely. It is 16 more miles to the watching beach and the road is often crossed by trucks and truck routes.

21.6   Arrive at rocky beach with sign announcing National Park. During February and March whales are consistently seen and may also be observed in January and April. Allow an entire half day for the drive in, viewing, and the drive out. Other routes should be used with great caution since the government and the salt company are trying to discourage their use and to encourage the single-entry road described.

Roads: Class II and III.

SARAFAN DUNES

0   At the Pemex station below the 138-foot-high steel eagle. Proceed straight north.

2.4   Take side road left into dry marsh. Road is not suitable for motorhomes, though it is possible for them to make it in and out. It is suitable for a two-wheel-drive auto if driven with caution and care. It is narrow, one-lane, but enjoys good visibility, is short and usually dry.

2.9   Keep right. Road left is to fisherman's hut.

3.6   Keep right. Occasionally a dune reaches this point and crosses the road. Without 4WD it might be best to walk the remaining distance.

3.8   Keep right. Road left goes to muddy beach.

4.2   T intersection at edge of tidal flats. Road left goes to fishermen's hut. Keep right for dunes.

4.4   Arrive at edge of high dunes. Park with care: ground insecure. Walk to first dune is 50 feet. Climb to top, about 300 feet. Do not enter without water or a companion. It is possible to become lost.

Roads: Class II and III.

A FORGOTTEN CITY

Cedros: I was alone in the cantina of the El Presidente Motel at the Oasis of Cataviña, in 1974, when near me sat down a tech-rep, a breed of man well described in detail by James Michener in *The Drifters*. We talked, and when he learned what I was doing he said:

"There's a town you've probably never heard of, and you should see it."

"Which town is that?"

"Cedros."

"And where is it?"

"On an island. You have to fly there—and maybe in a cargo plane. But there're three thousand people over there perched on the side of a big mountain in the prettiest little city you'll see in Baja. And not one American. Not one tourist of any kind."

Since the tech-rep's earlier conversation indicated he was not a man to exaggerate, in fact was probably one to understate, I pressed him for what he knew of Cedros.

"What does it cost to get there?"

"About fifteen dollars American for the round trip. Less than twenty, anyway."

When I was next in Guerrero Negro I lost little time in following up on the tech-rep's tip. In the main part of Guerrero Negro I found the office of Aero-Cali and purchased a ticket. I could not believe it would go smoothly, but it did.

This convair 440 twin-engine cargo/passenger plane loads for a 7:30 a.m. departure for Cedros Island at the Guerrero Negro Airport.

A 20-passenger twin-engine Convair, a combination cargo and passenger plant, was loaded promptly at 7:30 AM for its daily flight. It lifted off the short field at Guerrero Negro at 8 AM on schedule into a sky of low gray clouds. The pilot flew straight out to sea over Scammon's Lagoon, offering an excellent view of the Sarafan Dunes, the town of Guerrero Negro, and the hostile peninsula to the southwest, its coast described as the best beachcombing spot in the world.

The 120-mile flight over the Pacific takes less than an hour, and we arrived close to 8:30 in the morning. On the island, which is 20 miles long and ranges from five to 10 miles in width, there are wild goats, deer, and mountain lion as well as springs and forests of cedar trees from which the island takes its name.

The plane flew low over the city announcing its arrival and a swarm of red cabs began the 12 mile run out to the airfield on the southern tip of the mountainous island.

Because Scammon's Lagoon is too shallow for loading salt into oceangoing vessels, the salt is lightered out to Cedros Island, where in huge piles it awaits the Japanese freighters.

The city of Cedros on Cedros Island serves as a shipping point for salt mined in Guerrero Negro and as a fishing village for the small fleet operating there.

But the town is also a busy fishing port, particularly for shrimp. There is also a large steel fabricating plant as well as other light industries associated with the shipping of salt and the harvesting and processing of ocean products.

The cab fare for the eight-mile ride to town is 25 pesos ($1.25). Although the sun was high, the town was still asleep, quiet, not yet humming. Having been dropped in front of what the cabby said was a cafe, I pushed cautiously on the screen door. A young man led me to the back of a kitchen in a home. There a long table was set with a red and white checkered table cloth.

The three men already seated greeted me politely, subduing their curiosity about a red-bearded gringo. We were served Juevos Mexicana: an omelette, frijoles, and tortillas patted out on the oven next to us.

The men were a cannery foreman, a bank executive in suit and tie, and the owner of an insurance office.

Over the coffee and eggs we discussed Cedros—its lack of tourists, its anonymity, and its possible future. After three cups of coffee we parted. The breakfast was 20 pesos ($1).

Outside the home, called Cafe Betty, I stretched and began to walk away. Two young boys aged about 10 attached themselves to me. Francisco and Raul remained with me all day, alternately acting as guides and enjoying the spectacle of the Yankee with the strange American accent. They were concerned that I saw what I wanted to see, and that their friends *saw them* with me. It was a fair deal, since they were active and alert and at no time demanded money or hinted that they should be paid. They appeared to be extending their efforts as much for the interesting experience of watching and listening to a gringo and as a common courtesy on their small island home. During the day we drank Pepsis together and when I left I gave them each a dollar.

Francisco and Raul walked with me up the mountain to the springs to photograph the town far below. They stayed nearby and directed me to the city center, the customs agent—"He likes to talk to gringos, to speak English"—to the doctor, the mayor, and to various stores and hotels.

The hotel rooms we peeked into were 50 pesos for a single and 125 pesos for a double. In the U.S. they would be called "rustic." They did have plumbing and the water was occasionally heated. We walked along the main street and watched a mainland vendor, who had been on my flight, as he sold jewelry to the local teenage girls and boys.

We worked our way down to the wharves and large docks and photographed some shrimp boats. We were surprised to run into three Americans on the long dock. They had traveled down from San Diego to fish for yellow-tail, when the engine in their yacht had broken down and they had pulled in for repairs.

In the post office we bought stamps and received more stamps in change; in the grocery our change was store candy. We lounged on the sidewalk of the main street and watched a group of boys and girls playing hopscotch. After an afternoon bowl of soup I took a cab back out to the airport and at 4:30 caught the same plane I had come over on. Our first stop on the way back to Guerrero Negro was at Bahia Tortugas. There was no time to enter the city, but the air view of the fine, tiny round bay and tiny town on the parched peninsula was striking. The large aircraft was landed easily on the dirt strip in the style used by Alaska bush pilots. Indeed, while supplies were being unloaded and I looked out the round windows at the people of Tortugas and Cedros, I had the same sensations as when watching groups of people in the isolated towns of Alaska and Canada. The truck unloading supplies stalled beneath the wing and we passengers filed off the aircraft and pushed it out of the way prior to takeoff.

We lifted away from Tortugas, leaving a scene of white yachts lying gently at anchor in the clear blue waters of the bay. We were back in Guerrero Negro by 5:30 PM, behind me a day I would never forget.

Tickets are one-way to Cedros Island, for 125 pesos ($6 American). At Cedros a ticket is purchased for the return flight at the same price. Don't worry about getting left on Cedros, although the flights are generally full. If the ticket is purchased early (before 10 AM), there is no trouble. And if you have to spend a night the plane will be back the next day and you will have a good story to tell when you get back home.

In the mornings it is a different story. The passengers were called on board the plane in the order in which they had purchased tickets. So it is best to buy your ticket the day before you plan to fly. I bought mine about 15 minutes before boarding time and for a few moments, as I set atop some potato sacks, it appeared I would not go. A woman gave me her young boy's seat, he sat on my lap, and we left. No other Americans or tourists of any kind were on the aircraft either coming or going, and the pilot said he recalled none.

There is more to do on Cedros Island than I could do in one relaxed day occupied with taking photographs. A road crosses to the other side of the island, where several fishing camps dot the shore. There is

good potential for hiking and photography. The mountain behind the city rises 4000 feet above the sea, about the same height as all the mountains along the island. They are often in clouds.

Be careful: After you have been to Cedros Island and its city you may not rest until you return there. The high mountains, the beaches, the fishing boats, the clouds drifting over, the trails to explore, and the wildlife to seek all combine to make Cedros, if forgotten by the rest of the world, a very special Baja place.

There is no road-log for this section.

THE REMOTE

Abreojos: Reaching the dusty, windswept little village and abalone cannery of Abreojos is the first step into Baja's largest wilderness: the barren brown peninsula of the dry Vizcaino Desert, a terrain of mountain, salt flats, and sand dunes.

North on Mex 1 from San Ignacio, it is 72 miles and five hours to the village of 350 people on a lonely tip of land jutting into the Pacific. And both north and south from Abreojos, gray beaches stretch in a seemingly unbroken march of flat, hard sand and breakers.

Abreojos is a working village. The people live in small pastel-color dwellings arranged in nearly straight rows. They expect no tourists, receive few, and are prepared to cater to none. There is one hotel, Pedro Zuniga's house, one tiny, three-table cafe, the Cafe Elena. Both being no more than extensions of homes they are small and designed for Mexican travelers. As in so many other small Baja villages, the lone tourist is a curiosity; stares are common, as are rapid questions in Spanish and good-natured offers of assistance.

With proud fishermen, a small fleet of seagoing skiffs, the abalone cannery, a store, a landing strip, and the inevitable billiard parlour, Abreojos is a lively village. New homes and buildings are going up with a sweeping view of the Pacific; the cannery is clanging

The beach at Campo Rene near Abreojos (Openeyes).

and banging most of each day; and, like the rest of Baja, Abreojos enjoys a case of acute optimism.

Fuel and water are available. Gasoline is pumped by hand from black 55-gallon drums and then siphoned carefully into customers' tanks. Prices for food, gasoline, and lodging are the same that you paid in San Ignacio.

A two-wheel vehicle can complete the journey to Abreojos, but the road in can be difficult to follow, with many confusing turnoffs and divergences. With the exception of one lonely rancho 10 miles in, it is totally unpopulated. One enters this hostile peninsula prepared or does not enter at all. However, if you break down on this stretch, there is no reason to worry: Several vehicles a day travel in each direction.

Although it is 20 miles shorter and much flatter, the salt flats route should be rejected by all but the experienced. The flats appear solid and dry but their quicksand-like mixture of sea and earth swallows vehicles. The risk is too great for the distance saved. A Baja adage is fitting here: "A Mexican would rather travel two miles on a road he knows than one mile on one he doesn't know."

Beyond Abreojos the gravel road stretches another 150 miles through Asuncion and Tortugas, and on to Punta Eugenia where the peninsula ends.

One can make it in and out of Abreojos in one day, but it is better to stay overnight and take two. And although the whole trip to the end of the road at Punta Eugenia takes two days in and two days out, doing it in that short a time invites accident. (Attempting to do it in anything less invites disaster.)

The road to Abreojos is gravel all the way with a

few bad stretches of really troublesome big rocks. Grading is sporadic but there are no bad grades, hills, or arroyos requiring four-wheel-drive. In the States the road to Abreojos would be a bad road with a capital B. In Baja it is a good road.

Expect Class II generally on the road to Abreojos with some Class III and a rare section of Class IV.

MILE   SAN IGNACIO TO ABREOJOS

0   Secure gasoline at San Ignacio, proceed north 10.2 miles from highway Pemex at Parador on Mex 1 to sign inscribed "Fischer's Cafe." The left turn into the desert at 10.2 is not otherwise noted. The sign may also read "Fischer's Camp," depending on who last painted it.

10.2   Left turn into desert is off Mex 1. It is 62 miles of rocky desert road from here to Abreojos via the high road. The beginning of the road is rough, but improves after 7 miles.

16.5   Road begins to improve but continues to wind on a clear track west toward the Pacific Ocean over low desert hills and through a cactus and rock landscape. Far to the north and west the first outlines of the Santa Clara mountains begin to take shape.

19.9   Rancho San Angelo is a small, worn building with a corral and livestock grazing nearby. Riders are sometimes seen out working the cattle. This is a lonely, dry arroyo, with no services of any kind and could be mistaken for an abandoned rancho.

20.5   *Important Junction:* .6 beyond rancho. Salt Flat route to the left on the Y intersection, high road (recommended) to the right. Each road appears equally used because of the daring of the experienced and the knowledgeable truckers. There are no signs.

26.5   A branch enters from the left from the salt flats route.

27.8   Homemade sign announces proximity of the small Rancho El Rodeo. No services.

31.5   Another road comes in from the left from the salt flats route. The road goes almost due north, and the mountains ahead become clearer. Several side roads, which show less use, should be ignored and careful attention given to the route showing the most use. Sometimes the side roads reenter later and parallel the main route for several miles.

48.5   After 17 miles of winding over low hills a ridge is topped. Some road construction.

57.0   Moving due west now toward Pacific Ocean. A road branches left to flats route.

63.7   A well-used left branch goes to Campo Renee (deserted) .9 of a mile. The road is flat, camping is possible behind a low rise before the wide, clear beach. Shells are abundant. There are no trees, brush, or shelters of any kind.

65.7   Branch left to same beach.

70.0   Small group of dwellings on low rise, El Coyote. Lighthouse visible to right. Go through this tiny village, drop down to airstrip, parallel it, drive into Abreojos which is set overlooking ocean.

72.0   Arrive Abreojos. Road continues north to La Bocana at east edge of village.

This Log: Class III and IV.

MAGDALENA

Magdalena Bay: As the eye moves carefully down the long map of Baja California it settles inevitably on two bays: the one on the Sea of Cortez, well known, beautiful; and the other on the undeveloped west coast. A spark of hope is lit. Will the second bay be the equal of the first? Will Magdalena be as dramatic and inviting as Concepcion?

The hope sparked by the flat lines of a map is unfortunate. The two big bays are not at all alike. Although each is the dominant natural feature in its region, and each is enclosed by sharp projections of the coastline, there all similarity ends.

The Bay of Concepcion is part of the relatively quiet Sea of Cortez, and the second is a part of the ever-aroused Pacific Ocean. Concepcion can be embraced by the eye and its beginning and end, if indeed very large, can be easily imagined, but Magdalena defies the imagination, and no eye or telescope can take it all in.

Concepcion Bay is a clear, well-delineated jewel of green and blue waters set over white sands at the foot of rough, dry, steep mountains with an uncluttered shore reminiscent of Lake Tahoe.

Magdalena, 10 times larger, is less well defined, possesses a Pacific personality (fog and cold wind, large mudflats and strong currents) and consists primarily of sheltered, undramatic, gentle shores suited best to shallow-water sportfishing and waterfowl nesting and hunting. Magdalena is protected not by a prominent outthrust of land, as is Concepcion, but by a 150-mile-long string of offshore islands, some large, some small.

Magdalena's potential as a future recreation site is unlimited. Magdalena Bay is a sleeping giant, one that, for several reasons, will not be awakened soon. The major reason is its inaccessability. Because there are so few ways to reach it, and because it has no facilities, as a recreation and tourist place Magdalena simply does not exist.

There are no tourist pressure to develop the bay and very little is published about the bay that might increase interest. Magdalena is now used by the government and by the people only to harvest its natural resources and for subsistence.

The bay has countless hidden waterways that reach far inland and are protected from the Pacific by the long string of islands. Prior to World War II certain of these islands were used by the U.S. Navy as a gun-nery range. Much earlier, in 1871, several shiploads of American dreamers attempted to colonize the hostile interior adjacent to the bay. They left behind no mark; nothing on the waterless plain to suggest they were ever there. The colony was such a dismal failure that after 12 months it was abandoned and the Americans returned to the United States.

In contrast, the earliest land grant by the Mexican government in Baja was made in 1820, to the owners of Las Mantancitas, also adjacent to Magdalena. Located just south of Puerto Lopez Mateos, the Mexican ranch persists to this day.

Aside from the great Magdalena Island, which is over 50 miles long and one to 10 miles wide, and the thousands of miles of indented shoreline, the other major physical feature of the bay is the deepwater port of Puerto San Carlos.

This cotton-shipping port has large warehouses and docks. Behind the area, on the dull gray and green flats, is a tiny gathering of buildings that make up the town of 500 persons—one Pemex station, a grocery, a cafe, a billiard parlor, and several small modern government buildings.

Puerto San Carlos is a lonely place, and unless you go there to fish the flats when the tide is in, or to observe the cotton bales and docks or a chance freighter, there is little to see and do. On the other hand, it is a quiet place, and some motorhomes have parked peacefully there in groups of two or three from time to time.

The road in is paved and the distance short—38 miles each way. A Mexican sailor at a guard post waves most visitors directly onto the large docks, where the view of the immense bay is impressive. Sea ospreys are common and nest along the paved road near the port.

The first modern explorer to see Magdalena was Francisco de Ulloa in the service of Cortez in 1538. The next, 64 years later, was Sebastian Vizcaino, and a 100 years after that, in 1718, Jesuit missionaries rejected the area as a mission site.

A villager stops for a morning chat.

More than 200 years after that, in 1936, the Mexican government established a naval base at Puerto Cortez on Isla Margarita, at the southern end of the bay.

In the 40 years and more since, Bahia Magdalena has remained unchanged. Since its discovery it has seen occasional commercial use, but nothing else. On the great island the small town of Magdalena persists with 200 people. It is reached by both aircraft and boat from Puerto San Carlos. Puerto Cortez to the south has 300 people and Puerto Alcatraz, also on Isla Margarita, has 100 villagers.

North of Puerto San Carlos is the little cannery town of Lopez Mateos. From Villa Insurgentes, on Mex 1, a wide, graded, Class I and II dirt road runs west to Lopez Mateos. There is a landing strip and access to the quiet waterways; there are also a service station, motel, and grocery store. Over a 1000 people live in Lopez Mateos, and its small square and government buildings confirm it as a thriving town.

MILE   **PUERTO SAN CARLOS**

0 At large Pemex station in Ciudad Constitucion, facing north, drive back out of city toward Villa Insurgentes. Road angles left at major intersection with road sign indicating Puerto San Carlos.

.5 Left turn on paved road. Road proceeds straight west over low, rolling hills past farmlands to tidal flats.

6.7 Dirt road right is old road to Ejido Benito Juarez. This road proceeds north to the road between Villa Insurgentes and Puerto Lopez Mateos.

9.3 Road right proceeds north to road between Villa Insurgentes and Puerto Lopez Mateos and is the shorter route, not passing through Ejido Benito Juarez. This route is via Mantancitas, an old rancho.

35.0 Road from right proceeds north to Lopez Mateos through coastal flats. A concrete bridge is just ahead.

37.0 Road enters San Carlos after long sweeping turn below dike. Straight ahead for docks and left for town.

PUERTO LOPEZ MATEOS

0 At large Pemex station in Villa Insurgentes. This station is reached when coming south by turning right off Mex 1 into Villa Insurgentes and spotting the large station on the left, or west side, of the main street. Proceed north from this large station as if leaving town north on the dirt road.

.6 North of town on dirt road. A graded dirt road goes left into the irrigated countryside. These green fields and country roads with an occasional large tree are similar in appearance to the San Joaquin Valley of California.

7.0 Watch for cattle guard going west. The road will angle more toward the sea and leave the fertile areas for the less attractive desert.

22.0 You will have been moving over rolling, desolate desert on a good road. There is a curve to the right and the road going left goes to Puerto San Carlos.

23.0 Arrive at the town square of Lopez Mateos.

24.0 Arrive at the cannery gate and airport to right.

These Logs: Class II and III.

PUERTO CHALE

Puerto Chale is a lonely group of fishing huts where about 50 men, women, and children live on a still inlet on the southern end of Magdalena Bay. Mangrove lines the shore and the brown beach is muddy. Fishing nets hang for repair and across the water is the dim outline of Magdalena Island.

Just beyond Puerto Chale is the even tinier fishing

At the small village of El Datil on Magdalena Bay boats rest in small cove.

village of El Datil, where the road dead-ends. Here the shells of many turtles are imbedded with other debris in the beach mud.

Both fishing villages are within easy driving distance of Ciudad Constitucion or may be visited as side trips on the way to La Paz. They offer the easiest unpaved access to Magdalena Bay south of Puerto Lopez Mateos and boat launching from an auto trailer would be possible.

There are no facilities of any kind at either village, but their proximity to Ciudad Constitucion and the store and cafe at Santa Rita make facilities unnecessary. Expect Class II with some III on the way to Puerto Chale, and Class II and III from Puerto Chale to El Datil.

MILE MEX 1 TO PUERTO CHALE & EL DATIL

0   **At Santa Rita Village on Mex 1, 35 miles south of Ciudad Constitucion. Make a right turn, west, toward Magdalena Bay. There is usually a sign.**

3.9 **Summit, ahead see Rancho Medano and new schoolhouse.**

4.5 **Medano, watch gully and deep dust straight ahead.**

4.8 Pass through ranch-village to left and drop into gully, where some deep holes are hidden by dust. Class IV upgrade.

5.0 Road tops out on plain and runs west to Magdalena Bay. Some ruts and turnouts, stay on main road west. Class II.

14.0 Puerto Chale, an ejido, is by the bay. Road winds into gathering of poor huts and dead-ends at muddy beach with mangrove to right and left and many inlets and lagoons in general area.

About 100 yards before the road to the beach dead-ends, there is a road to the left. It leads to El Datil. If you take the left:

15.0 Wind through sand dunes on firm Class II base with some rutted III. Bay is to right.

16.0 Pass over flat, sandy, brushy plain and drop into small cove with several huts and tiny beach. This is El Datil and here the road again dead-ends.

Expect Class II and III to Puerto Chale with more II and one Class IV gully at Medano.

Expect Class II and III from Puerto Chale to El Datil, with more III.

THE LONELINESS LOOPS

El Conejo North and South: Beginning 12 miles north of La Paz, four roads go west from Mex 1 to the Pacific coast. All are occasionally used by campers and ranchers, but some are in much worse condition than others.

The fourth road, about 50 miles north of La Paz, offers access to the entire area and is the favorite because the distance from turnoff to sea is a short nine miles and the road is in relatively good shape.

With repeated use of El Conejo by surfers, some homemade signs have appeared, and it is becoming easy to find. Its beach is open but contains many rocks. The big breakers roll in with a good wave, the fishing is fair, the camping undisturbed. The wind blows regularly but is gentlest in November and December.

A white-earth road twists its way north from Conejo, hugging the dunes and shore. The road south, although rockier, is in better condition due to heavier use. Both are lonely trips, and both loop back to the blacktop. The road south does not require four-wheel-drive, while the one north does. The run north is 40 miles and takes four hours; the road south is 30 miles and takes three hours.

The narrow path north amidst low brush beside the windswept sea, evokes a sense of loneliness and desolation that can prove a sobering experience. The nine miles from the blacktop to the sea are Class II and III. At El Conejo there is good parking and turnaround space. The Rancho El Conejo itself is one mile south. Autos can safely travel this first nine miles, but should not be taken on either of the two alternate exits.

The road north leads past fine lonely beaches not seen by many people. Where it loops back toward the blacktop, the road passes through green irrigated ranch land. This stretch is an ideal challenge to equipment and skills, because it deteriorates to Class VIII and IX. In the final miles before Mex 1 it passes through the scourge of Baja, the thick chalky silt so fine that it settles like water in the road-way holes, hiding them, and billowing in the air at impact like a thick fog.

I once took a wrong turn on the north road which led me several miles over rocky hills to a place where the road dead-ended at a stone hut and stone corral holding an emaciated little goat. A Mexican man, all smiles, came out to the sound of the Honda and behind him followed his wife, her hand shielding her eyes from the burning sun.

I was low on gas and angry with myself for having become lost. In Spanish I said that I was lost and

---

South of El Conejo (The Rabbit) the road moves over the lonely landscape toward La Paz.

THE LONELINESS LOOPS

needed his help. He replied that he would help me but first I must sit and rest and take food and coffee with him and his wife. He could see that I was tired, he said, and after I had eaten he would draw me a map in the sand.

Their rock hut was no more than 10 by 12 feet, but the obvious concern and the natural dignity of the two people confronting me with warm smiles on the rocky slope upon which they were conducting their lives had a calming effect.

"I insist," his wife said in Spanish. "You take coffee and beans with us."

I removed my helmet, bent over and entered their hut, sat down, and was served. Thirty minutes later the man told me where I was and how to find my way back to the carretera. And I felt, as I had so many times in the past on the backroads of Baja, that it would be an insult not to accept hospitality offered. It's so easy to get lost on Baja's back roads that you have to learn to save room for the coffee that will be offered and to remember the latest news from La Paz or Tijuana.

When the coffee was down and the beans consumed the handshaking took place in front of the hut. The handshake, in Mexican style, was not firm and strong, but a light slipping together of the hands with a slight momentary pressure of the thumbs.

MEX 1 NORTH OF LA PAZ TO EL CONEJO AND NORTH
MILE

After traveling 45.6 miles north of La Paz on Mex 1, look for the tiny restaurant at San Agustin on the left. Proceed 2.4 miles north of San Agustin to left turn for El Conejo. The same turn is 1.3 miles south of El Coyote Microwave Station tower. Set trip gauge at 0 at turnoff.

0

4.9 Five miles in you reach the top of a small summit and begin to drop to the sea. The road is rocky and narrow but easily negotiable. Campers and vans should have no trouble; it is a questionable route for mo-

torhomes of any size. A passenger auto driven with care and with high clearance could go the 9 miles without damage.

9.2 Here the sea is close and visible about a quarter-mile straight ahead. This is a *three-way fork*. Go left .5 mile for the beach and parking close to the ocean. Go straight ahead .2 mile for parking in the large overlook area. Turn right at this point to continue north up the coast and left to continue south. This log goes north from 9.2

13.9 Firm sandy road leads through dunes to various arroyos and tiny fishing camps. Various roads to beach .2 mile.

15.4 Road forks right to rancho out of sight. Go straight.

19.5 Road forks left to beach. Here main route leaves beach and moves inland 2 miles.

21.4 Road forks right to rancho out of sight. Go straight.

22.0 Cement-block structure abandoned on right. Pass through green arroyo with high willows. Cattle abundant.

22.6 Swing back to beach and then leave again.

23.4 Road forks right to rancho out of sight. Go straight.

25.6 Beach road to left .7 mile to beach.

28.9 *Major Fork:* A right turn is essential here. All the road appears equally good and equally well used, but to continue straight ahead from here is to wallow a few miles distant in deep sand dunes.

30.6 Afer the right turn at the major fork the road swings inland about 2 miles. To the right green fields and a fence appear. At 30.6 there is a gate and in the distance a ranch. Open the gate and go through and close it again. Proceed straight ahead and on the right will be Rancho Sacrificio. If there are people around you may want to confirm where you are and where you are going. Ask for Penjamo, the little place where the loop exits on the highway. You can also indicate Ciudad Constitucion or La Paz, or simply the blacktop by saying "carretera." This should get you accurate directions.

31.8 You should be at a second gate. There is a gathering of dwellings on the left. Open the gate, go through, close it and keep right. You will enter now the area of deep, dry, powdery silt. Drive slowly. The silt hides the holes. What appears to be a level dirt road is not. The silt lasts for 6 miles. Various roads meander off left and right and this route forks in many places to avoid the worst holes. Many of the side routes return ahead but try to keep on the main road.

37.4 Leave deep silt and begin climbing out of valley. Top a rocky plateau and move north.

38.0 *Major Fork:* A broken sign lies on the ground. Ignore it. The main road appears to go to the right, but it goes to Rancho Santa Maria. Keep left or straight ahead. Road will begin to angle east toward the blacktop.

42.7 Reach blacktop at small village of Penjamo. Gas available from drums. Small cafe. No lodging.

There are no service stations between Ciudad Constitucion and La Paz, a distance of 140 miles, but some of the villages along the way will have gasoline for sale from 55 gallon drums.

Roads are Class II and III, occasional IV.

MILE LA PAZ TO EL CONEJO AND SOUTH

0 At El Conejo 9 miles in from blacktop.

1.8 Branch left, keep straight.

2.5 Rock corral and group of trees to left.

2.6 Fork right to beach .2.

2.8 Fork right to beach .2.

5.8 Rancho to left, palms in valley, beach to right.

8.0 Class IV down .3.

9.2 Beach, lagoon, fishing camp.

9.6 Road left to blacktop 15 miles.

11.2 Column of stones with stake in center on beach right.

12.4 Rancho left, palms in valley, keep to right.

13.5 View of beach more than 10 miles long, rock monument left, wreck of old iron ship to right on beach.

14.7 Gathering of poor huts, Rancho Costa Azul. Road begins to move away from beach areas.

18.4 Fork right to beach 4 miles.

19.5 Long straight stretch of Class II road leading into sharp turns.

20.5 Long straight stretch of Class II road.

30.0 Cross arroyo.

31.5 Abandoned rancho right.

33.5 Reach blacktop opposite highway sign reading El Sacrificio at point .2 mile north of El Metape microwave station and 21 miles south of cafe San Augustin.

Expect Class II and III on this run with some IV.

AN UNSPOILED SUR

Cabo San Lucas North on the Pacific: The last stretch of Baja's Pacific coast is the best. The road north from Cabo San Lucas to Todos Santos, a dirt-road alternative to the blacktop return to La Paz, will

The Sierra de la Laguna are visible from the summit at mile 14.6 on the road to Todos Santos.

reveal a portion of these unspoiled Pacific beaches. And at Todos Santos there is again pavement.

The drive down to Land's End from La Paz seems to be a compulsive act, so, many tourists end up at the tiny town of Cabo San Lucas wondering what to do next and if they should attempt the dirt road to Todos Santos.

The road meandering out of the little community toward the airport and municipal dump is an unassuming dusty, narrow path. And most tourists decide against it and return to La Paz the same way they came, by the 139 miles of Mex 1 blacktop. For tourists in an ordinary passenger auto that is the wise decision.

Although most of the 56-mile-long dirt road from Cabo to Todos Santos is easily negotiable Class II and III, there are a few troublesome sections of Class IV that can damage low-clearance autos. It is, however, an exciting, rewarding stretch of mountain road spotted by enough remote beaches to make it extremely attractive. There is no gas, food, or lodging between Cabo and the villages just south of Todos Santos, so plan on being on your own for 40 miles if you start in here.

The beaches midway, easily reached by auto, offer many good camping and fishing spots.

MILE   **CABO SAN LUCAS NORTH VIA TODOS SANTOS ROAD**

0   **At Cabo San Lucas Plaza. The turnoff for Todos Santos is north of town .2 of a mile, just south of the Pemex station. It is a left turn and is often unmarked. Proceed west out of Cabo through adobe and wood-hut neighborhoods until the road widens into a**

Class I graded stretch. It climbs steadily uphill away from Cabo San Lucas; behind you are some good views of land's end.

3.5 Rancho Sante Fe to left, large handmade sign.

5.0 City dumps to left.

5.5 *Major Intersection:* Straight ahead for airport. Right for Todos Santos. Road narrows beyond this point and becomes high centered with sand until the mountain grades begin. Expect about 7 miles of hard-packed sand-based, one-way road. Traffic is almost always light, so meeting more than one or two trucks or autos is uncommon.

11.5 Fork right to El Sauzal, marked with sign. Keep straight.

12.0 Fork left to Los Pozos, no sign. A gathering of huts .2 mile in and the entrance to additional beaches requiring 4WD.

12.5 High center road continues and canyon narrows as road enters mountains. No steep grades, some sharp turns.

12.8 Fork left, go left. Right goes to Rancho Candelaria.

14.6 Summit with turnout. View of Pacific below, high Sierra de La Laguna to right and north. Road drops down steeply from here.

22.0 First view of beach and breakers near El Migriño. From here road improves. Some damage from 1976 hurricane will remain for several months as repair is progressing slowly.

23.6 Rancho with large well on left.

23.9 Sharp left for first accessible beach. Keep straight for main road.

25.3 Beach to left. Good camping sites, plenty of turnouts. One of the nicest spots on this road. Road leaves beach ahead.

35.0 Road returns to sea after 8 miles inland.

35.3 Beach to left. Fine camp site, cave in sea rocks to left.

37.6 Enter small village of Plutarco. Gas and supplies available. Cafe and grocery on main road. Drive slowly.

40.4 Swing back to beach and proceed over low summit. The views are impressive but camping here is not as good as that to the south because of proximity to villages.

53.4 Enter village of Pescadero. There is a detour in preparation for the coming blacktop. A short stretch of blacktop begins ahead and then ends in Todos Santos.

56.0 Enter Todos Santos, continue to T intersection, then right turn straight through to blacktop leading to La Paz.

Expect Class II and III on this run with minimal IV, but use caution in 12-mile area of high center road and potentially deep sand.

FORGOTTEN SUR

Cabo San Lucas to El Migriño via San Cristobal: West of the road to Todos Santos lies a string of beaches that are accessible by road, but are known to very few people, as are the partially hidden roads leading to them.

On my first trip to the beautiful crescent of San Cristobal I remember taking in the sweep of the white sands and gentle beach, as photographer Robert Western pointed to the fresh and unmistakable trail of a thousand-pound sea turtle. Her tracks led from the ocean over the sand to wherever she had crawled with determination to deposit her eggs.

Beside us was a deserted modern building about 100 feet long and one storey high. Inside it, still intact, were offices, dormitories, a dining room and

kitchen, and some displays of marine life. Below it on the beach was a large cement collection tank. The site no longer in use, was a branch of the University of Mexico's Marine Studies Institute. It was reached only by sea. Arriving by land was an unusual way to visit.

There are two ways to penetrate the mountains north of Cabo San Lucas to find this hidden and almost forgotten stretch of Pacific coast.

The first, through Los Pozos off the road to Todos Santos, allows a loop in to San Cristobal and back to the Todos Santos road just north of El Migriño. This route is strictly for four-wheel-drive since it is virtually unused. Many parts of its 10 miles to the beach are real hair-raisers, but once traveled it holds less fear.

The second route is easier: Directly out of Cabo San Lucas toward the lighthouse, called El Faro in Spanish, it is on a route marked with signs for the "Baja 200," a La Paz-sponsored race for cycles, autos, and dune buggies.

It is 13 miles to San Cristobal beach and the adjacent ranch of the same name. The road to the beach terminates at the ranch, but about .2 of a mile from the ranch there is a dim track over to the former Marine Studies Institute. Off that track there is a second dim trail to a gully leading to the beach. Following this course, one can drive to the white sands of San Cristobal and away from the ranch for private camping.

Stop and ask permission at the ranch. It's a way of introducing yourself and being polite.

I can't guarantee a sea turtle here, or at the equally beautiful beaches that continue on in greater isolation north of San Cristobal. But the beach does have a magic feeling, and who knows what lies south of it on the totally untouched miles back to Land's End?

At mile 6.2 beyond Los Pozos, Rancho Agua Escondido comes suddenly into view. The bricks were hauled from San José Del Cabo over 50 dirt miles away.

CABO SAN LUCAS TO EL MIGRIÑO VIA SAN CRISTOBAL

MILE

Route 1

0 At Los Pozos, 12 miles north of Cabo San Lucas on the Todos Santos Road. Los Pozos, .5 mile beyond the right turn and sign for El Sauzal, is an unmarked left turn into the tall cactus. A gathering of dwellings around a large well is quickly reached; the road to the beach is hard to discover. It is to the left behind the big corral and down an old cattle trail and stream bed. About 300 yards down this trail a set of twin ruts will appear. Follow these west.

2.0 Top rise, granite outcrop to right, ocean view ahead, drop down into riverbed from this point.

3.0 Branch right to sea via ridge tops. Follow ridges down to rancho.

6.2 Rancho Agua Escondido with corral and brick house. Road comes in at corral, winds into yard, and cuts left away and back down into arroyo below house. Climb in and out, up to opposite ridge.

7.5 *Major Intersection:* T intersection, left for Cabo San Lucas, right for San Cristobal and route south to El Migriño. Rancho Agua Escondido is behind you on the other side of the ridge.

7.8 After going right at 7.5 you reach a four-way *major intersection:* Left is to Rancho Las Palmas just south of San Cristobal, right winds back out to Todos Santos road, and straight ahead goes to San Cristobal and route south to El Migriño. Sometimes a blue and white sign and cow skull point the way to San Cristobal.

8.6 Fork right to abandoned rancho .2. Go straight.

13.2 Fork right at beach to route south, go left at corral for San Cristobal.

13.3 Rancho San Cristobal, institute building to right above beach; dim track right is to Institute and beach.

13.6 Taking right turn at Cristobal, proceeding south to El Migriño, cross wide flat arroyo with beach to left; road deteriorates since it runs between two beach ranches that use other roads for access. Some boulders and cliffs for camping shelter ahead.

15.1 Long beach on left, large boulders, good camping. This area before the next ranch at 18 mile is the best spot along here.

15.3 Long beach on left, rocky point. Road winds in and out of narrow, short, steep arroyos, and four-wheel-drive is necessary. It is not rough, but it is steep and slippery; in four-wheel-drive it is a quiet, gentle drive with no rough rocks in evidence.

16.0 Leave beaches and wind uphill to ridge top. Spectacular views.

17.2 Road returns to beach to left.

18.0 Rancho Margarita. This is a tiny ranch on a large beach.

18.5 Rancho Pozo del Costa. This larger ranch is also on a large beach, in a grove of palms.

20.5 Connect with Todos Santos Road from Cabo San Lucas. Go left for El Migriño, about 2 miles.

CABO SAN LUCAS TO EL MIGRIÑO VIA SAN CRISTOBAL

Route 2

0 At plaza in Cabo San Lucas. Take a left within town and pass a modern school building on left through residential section.

1.1 Fork left, go left. Right proceeds to Todos Santos Road.

1.3 Fork left for El Faro (lighthouse), go right. "Baja 200" signs also indicate a right turn here.

3.5 Fork right. "Baja 200" signs say go left. Go left also for San Cristobal.

5.9 Fork left. Go left. "Baja 200" sign agrees.

7.7 Fork left. Go left. "Baja 200" sign agrees.

8.1 Rancho on road to right. Large cardon grove.

8.2 Drop into small arroyo, cross and climb out other side.

10.0 Top rise.

10.4 *Major Intersection:* Fork right goes to Rancho Agua Escondido; "Baja 200" signs point that way also. Go straight ahead for San Cristobal. This is where the route from Los Pozos comes in.

10.7 Four-way intersection: left to Las Palmas Rancho, right to Todos Santos Road, straight ahead for San Cristobal.

11.5 Fork right to abandoned rancho .2. Keep straight ahead.

16.1 Fork right to El Migriño, left to San Cristobal. You are at the beach and a corral is on your left. Go to Log of route 1 at mile 13.6 for continuation of this route.

CABO SAN LUCAS TO
MILE   THE LIGHTHOUSE (EL FARO)

0 At plaza in Cabo San Lucas. Follow same route out of town as route 2 to San Cristobal.

1.3 This second left fork is for El Faro. "Baja 200" sign indicates right. Go left for lighthouse.

1.4 Gate. Go through and close.

1.6 Fork left to rancho near beach. If proceeding left:

1.0 Rancho.

1.5 Winding by rancho come to lagoon and high sand dunes beyond which is an excellent beach leading back to Land's End. A long walk.

If proceeding straight at 1.6:

2.2 Fork left for El Faro. Road proceeds straight 3 miles to end of beach and ends in sand dunes.

3.0 4WD necessary here to get to lighthouse. Steep, rocky, sharp turns. Dim trail straight ahead off sharp curve is dune-buggy track to long beach south.

3.5 Lighthouse point and good views in all directions. Old lighthouse below near beach.

Expect Class VII and VIII on route 1 to San Cristobal.

Expect Class III and IV on route 2 to San Cristobal.

Expect Class III on route to lighthouse with Class VII last .5.

Expect Class VII and VIII San Cristobal to Todos Santos Road.

2

THE INTERIOR

"I have in me that fierce desire to learn what is on the other side of the hill, to know what is off the beaten track."

Erle Stanley Gardner,
Off the Beaten Track in Baja, 1967.

"Life is invariably good—provided the trail to the wilderness lies open."

A. W. North,
Camp and Camino in Lower California, 1910.

"From where I stood there was no visible evidence that the earth was inhabited."

Joseph Wood Krutch,
The Forgotten Peninsula, 1961.

"Don't you realize, señor, that out there it is easy to die?"

Santiago merchant Cirilio Gomez, 1975.

"If I die I hope I wake on that road to Mission Santa Maria, the first sun breaking on the tan mountains, the white, sandy, winding road moving out ahead of me."

Anonymous Baja traveler, 1974.

"In the year 1767 Padre Arnes established the Mission of Santa Maria . . . on a bench in a deep canyon . . . mountains rising on every side. . . . Indians lived near-by in nightly dread of vicious lions. . . . a forest of beautiful palms offered a delightful resting spot."

A. W. North,
The Mother of California, 1908.

NORTHEAST BAJA

Farm Frontier: Sprawling south and east of the city of Mexicali, this often overlooked area of eastern Baja encompasses 2500 square miles of rich irrigated farming country adjacent to California's own reclaimed land in the Imperial Valley.

The drive from Tijuana to Mexicali, Baja's two largest cities, is an easy 125 miles over paved road and is worth it for the awe-inspiring view and the steep grade just east of La Rumorosa, near the trip's halfway point. So sudden and dramatic is the descent from La Rumorosa, high among the pines, to the dry hot sands of Laguna Salada that no traveler can fail to be impressed. From there the drive into Mexicali is short and swift, if hot—plenty hot from May through August.

A visit to the small farming centers in the countryside is worth a day's ride out of Mexicali where there is a wide variety of crops and herds.

South of Nuevo Leon the road crosses what is left of the Colorado River when it reaches Mexico. It could easily be mistaken for an irrigation ditch. There are many service stations, tiny restaurants, and motels. But the area is not considered a tourist attraction —which is precisely why it is worth visiting.

The town of Coahuila is half in the Mexican State of Sonora and half in Baja California; it is also split by the Sonora–Baja Railroad. Each part also has its own police chief and municipal administration, and though it is almost impossible to observe where one

The great expanse of the desert is sobering.

54

half begins and the other ends, there is a spirit of competition between the two parts.

I once arrived in Coahuila in the company of two Mexican men, one a short plumber driving a yellow Ford pickup with appropriate tassles and the other a tall, hard-drinking friend of his. They had magnanimously loaded my motorcycle, stricken with some internal disease (later diagnosed as a bearing problem), into the rear of their pickup after coming upon me four o'clock one morning in the desert near Valle de Trinidad, in the Sierra Juarez. Why were they so far from home in the wee hours? On the spur of the moment they had engaged in a minor fiesta of cousins and aunts and uncles. Since they were on their way back to Coahuila when they found me, I had to go there, too.

And since each of them was from a different side of the town, their "lost yanqui" was hauled about and shown off with his "moto" to the chiefs and mayors of each town.

The actions of the little man and his large friend tell something about the people of Mexicali and the little towns like Coahuila located clear at the other end of the valley. The little man, Ramon, said, "We want to see our friends, we go see them," took a drink of beer, and slapped me on the back. And Luis, the larger, nodded agreement.

A truck before us braked but Ramon, driving, did not notice. Looking up from his talking at the last moment he didn't lose a breath, drove off the highway into a field to the right, taking out several fence posts, wrestled the pickup, bouncing violently, in and out of a small ditch, and then returned the truck to the pavement, saying, "Give me another beer, Jim."

Luis said, "No problem, Jim. Don't worry. No problem," and drank his own beer.

We ate lunch and they tried to kidnap a peacock from the restaurant barnyard, but the señora chased them away. During our meanderings about town they told me of themselves and the town. They said they had grown up in Coahuila. It was a good place, but everyone went finally to Mexicali or Tijuana. Why? For opportunity. Some men stayed in the fields and

that was fine, but they, Ramon and Luis, were plumbers, tradesmen; and although prices were high and the cost of electricity in their opinion prohibitive, they were happy.

Ramon and Luis are not always on a fiesta, but a trip to Baja's northeast requires no road-log to find its varied and interesting corners and its hard-working, hard-living people.

PALM SPRINGS

Cantu Palms: The names, the idea, the very sound of something like a hot springs and shading palms is a difficult lure to resist. The oases of Cantu and Guadalupe are at the eastern foot of the Sierra Juarez, high, swiftly rising, rocky red mountains that sparkle and reflect in the awful heat of the desert.

This is a tough, undeveloped place. The roads often lead nowhere, the signs, if up, are frequently misleading, the surface is sometimes terrible, sometimes excellent. But in case you were wondering, there is no end to possible adventure where desert and mountains meet.

A camper vehicle can get here, but there are no facilities. In fact, at the first spring marked on the map there is nothing—not even a spring. It has gone underground and so the palms still grow, but you must bring your own water.

Cantu Palms is worth exploring. There is a quartz miner's hut, an old road traversable only on foot, that climbs to an active quartz mine, and piles and piles of the white residue. It is 40 miles from Mexicali and 50 miles from La Rumorosa. Expect Class I and II roads with spots of III.

MILE   CANTU PALMS

At 66.4 miles east of Tecate on Mex 2 and 25 miles west of Mexicali there is, on the northern tip of Laguna Salada, a tiny Pemex station and adjoining outdoor cafe labeled "Servicio." It is here that the road

turns south into the desert. An alternative is to travel exactly 2.6 west of the Servicio toward La Rumorosa where a turnoff unmarked by a sign goes straight south into the desert toward Cantu Palms and Canon Guadalupe. At Servicio set trip gauge at 0 and turn onto this road. This is wide, graded, straight road, perfectly passable in the dry season, which is most of the time. For the first few miles a fence parallels the road to the left and to the right are the sharply rising rocky Sierra Juarez Mountains from which the springs come.

0

6.2 An old sign announces the Ejido (cooperative) el Tigre. Do not turn right. Continue straight ahead on the various tire tracks. Avoid the tracks too far to the left since there lies the dry lagoon, which is sometimes not so dry.

16.1 Maze of roads begins. Keep generally right. Come to a small ranch with livestock and pick up alternate road coming in along the foothills.

17.5 Past ranch, road turns right to Cantu Palms. Go in 1.5 miles on Class III road, last .5 mile is Class IV; advise walking up to palms and miner's hut. Actual mine is uphill along miner's road past the palm trees .5 mile where the road ends abruptly.

Expect Class I and II into Palms, but last .2 mile much rougher.

Canon Guadalupe: Beyond Cantu Palms is the real oasis of Canon Guadalupe, 40 miles from the highway over generally good roads that deteriorate quite near the springs. The drive in should take no more than two careful hours, perhaps less.

An enterprising member of the Arce family, one of Baja's oldest, charges $3 per vehicle to enter the property. There are no facilities—no store, no electricity, no place to purchase gasoline—so bring every-

Beyond Cantu Palms 2 miles a small quartz mine shelters a blue and white shrine to the Virgin of Guadalupe.

thing you want with you. The charge is for the right to use the water.

Directly past the gate to the left is a large natural swimming pool filled with the steaming water coming from the mountainside. A few campers are usually present.

Further in, on the slope of the rocky hill, are several natural, unimproved camping spots. Here there is room to park vehicles. Nearby is a natural pool of hot water in which to sink and feel the heat rest the body, the water wash away the desert dust.

After that, walk over to the stream bed and work upward to the former beauty spot, the pool of the virgin. Although it was filled with sand by a hurricane, it is still a remarkable spot. A thin stream of cold water escaping from the mountains continues to cascade gently over the lip of high rock, but now, sadly, into a bowl of sand.

MILE	CANON GUADALUPE

The road to Canon Guadalupe is the same as the one to Cantu Palms. Begin this log at 16.1 of the Cantu Palms log.

16.1 Maze of roads ends at rancho. Go left to Guadalupe.

17.5 Road right goes to Cantu Palms. No water.

Mine active, but usually no one there. The road continues here along the edge of the mountains. On the left the Laguna Salada is waterless and desolate. To the right are the high, very steep rocky mountains.

28.7 *Major Fork:* small sign for Guadalupe, go to sharp right. Do not turn right before this intersection. Prior right turns end at Canyon Tajo, where a trail once used by Indians on the way to gather piñon nuts climbs to the high plateaus at 6000 feet. It is no trail to attempt without someone who has been on it before and is best attempted from the mountains downward.

30.7 Now you have made a right turn and are heading generally west toward the mountains. The prominent peak to the left is Picacho Rasco, which is just above the Pool of the Virgin. At this point the road seems to branch right, but keep to the left. The branch returns ahead.

32.7 Similar fork. Keep left.

33.3 Fence and grafitti on rock. Road begins to go south along mountain.

34.0 First view of palm trees. Road begins to wind and to become rocky with some difficult series of rocks and sharp turns. 4WD not necessary but low-clearance vehicles and 2-wheel-drive autos will require great care to negotiate this stretch without damage.

35.6 White posts mark edge of Canon Guadalupe property.

36.0 Gate and pool. Pay $3 per vehicle.

Class I and II to 28.7; II to 34.0; III to 36.0.

Class II road at mile 37 near Laguna Hanson.

LAGUNA HANSON

Laguna Hanson: In the last century an American cattle rancher who lived and worked in Baja was shot and killed near this small, rare mountain lake. The place now bears his name.

It is a Mexican National Park, and the decision to protect it was a wise one. But amazingly, with all the natural beauty of its exciting mountains and pine trees, its relatively good road, and its excellent camping, it is probably visited on the average by no more than one tourist auto a day. The several times I've been there I have never seen any other Americans, nor any tourist of any kind.

The road runs in 40 miles from La Rumorosa to the lake. As an alternative to a round trip, the paved Highway Mex 16 is 20 more good downhill dirt miles beyond. From there it is 30 miles west to Ensenada or 40 south to Valle de Trinidad.

The hardpacked sandy road winds through the mountains around trees and great granite boulders like some scene out of a western film, and indeed from time to time a Mexican cowboy on horse or mule appears.

Near the lake is a forest service station where several men are on duty year-round to fight forest fires and maintain the road. Beyond the station, on a smaller lake adjoining Laguna Hanson, is a former boys' home, occupied by several families who work at the experimental tree farm a short distance further on.

Only a day's drive from San Diego this mountain pond near Laguna Hanson is without development and sees few visitors. In the past a boys' home was located here but now the structures are abandoned.

There are no facilities of any kind at Laguna Hanson: no gas, no food, no lodging. The lake itself, small and shallow, would be labeled a pond in the Sierra Nevada, but here, with its pines and boulders and high rocky ridge backing it, it merits its local prestige.

Aserradero: A few miles beyond Laguna Hanson is the small lumber town of Aserradero, where, at its one cafe with its single table, simple meals will be served to tourists, and where, if the need warrants a careful search, gasoline can be found.

But Aserradero deserves attention not for services but because, like no other village in the wood-starved land of Baja, it is built of logs and milled lumber. Like the road leading to it, it looks like part of the old west, and is a fine surprise.

LA RUMOROSA TO LAGUNA HANSON AND ASERRADERO

MILE

As is typical of Baja, the turnoff for Laguna Hanson should be easy to find but is not. It is not in La Rumorosa where it should be, but right next to a yellow building west of

the town. A big yellow and red sign there gives directions and distances. There is also a yellow cafe; all of this on the right if you are going east, just before you enter La Rumorosa. (La Rumorosa, which has a grocery store, and a service station, is where you should buy your supplies.) The cafe is called the Calera and the sign says, among other things: "Al Parque 50 kms." This place is 1 mile west of La Rumorosa and .5 miles east of the big Planta El Piñon.

0   At the Cafe Calera set your trip-guage at 0 and turn south (right if coming from the west, left if from La Rumorosa).

2.5   Rancho San Francisco. The road gently rises and falls here with few rocks and a good, partially limestone surface. You will be seeing signs with arrows for the big co-operative down the road. Ignore them; they are not for you.

3.5   Keep right even though arrow and sign point left. That is the road to the cooperative. You are in a large mountain meadow, green and beautiful throughout the year.

6.4   Steep hill, Class III.

7.4   Keep left as road seems to branch right.

12.3   Rancho La Ponderosa. Signs announce this. Some deep sand in road, but not enough to be dangerous. *Watch out for swift trucks of Mexican wood-gatherers.* They will run you into the cactus and end your trip, not from malice but the trucker's intensity, his mania to make the run as fast as possible. When this is mixed with the Mexican's natural wildness on mountain roads, *watch out.*

13.1   Go left for 2 mile alternate loop to Rancho Carmelo. 4WD only: 1.0, three-way intersection, go left; 1.9 rancho, corral, horses, small house, well; road loops back out to 13.9.

13.9   Road from Rancho Carmelo enters from left.

15.9   Road has continued to wind up and down and over low hills between tall pines and big boulders. Road enters from right.

17.0   Fork to right. Keep left, straight ahead.

22.3   Reach large high mountain meadow, land of Rancho El Topo. Fence to right; road seems to go into ranch house. You go left along fence and then out of valley over a high hill. Keep generally to the right.

24.5   Prepare for Class III and IV grade. .5 mile up.

25.0   Top.

26.5   Prepare to go up Class III and IV grade. .6 mile up.

27.1   Top.

29.2   Branch right, go straight ahead.

29.9   Fork to right, go left.

35.0   Ranger station, fire fighters, large buildings to right; tall pines, lake ahead to left.

38.1   Road branches off toward lake and small camping area in trees. Some tables. Water in lake not potable. Expect shore to be muddy and shallow. In extremely dry seasons lake contains no water. It has not been dry since 1973.

38.6   Park entrance and deserted office and buildings. Boys' camp buildings and second lake off to right in trees.

39.1   Experimental tree farm. Small buildings, 4 acres.

40.2   Second entrance to boys' home buildings and camp. Lake.

44.4   Enter village of Aserradero (pop.: 150), cafe on left, ball field to the right.

LAGUNA HANSON TO
MEX 16 BLACKTOP

MILE

If you don't wish to return the same way you came in to Laguna Hanson, use the following route, which begins in Aserradero. Set trip-gauge at 0 at Laguna Hanson campground.

0

4.2 Aserradero. Enter town, cross stream, go up hill to right, wind out of town south and west.

5.0 Long downgrade, good road; watch for trucks.

6.2 Road right, go left; branch joins later.

7.4 *Major Fork:* Branch to Rancho Catarina, to left, is alternate route to Mex 16—*not* recommended: many variations in route and much road deterioration. Often used by Baja motorcycle racers and speeding dune buggies. Beware. Keep right at this intersection.

8.8 Steep descent but graded road. This is a good stretch of winding mountain road to enjoy. You are leaving the high sierra for the big valley.

16.6 Large shade trees, good spot to pull over and rest. Old foundation and dangerous well. Don't fall in.

16.9 Fork left, go left for winding up-and-down route to Mex 16. Go right for Ojos Negros via dirt road .7 mile west.

21.2 After winding over hills and descending into the valley, reach blacktop "Carretera." There is a sign, "Galeria Pelayo 35 km," and a cattle guard and cattle gate. Your choice: left to Valle de Trinidad, a small farming center with gas and food and lodging but nothing fancy; or right to Ensenada, where, every 15 minutes of every workday, from 5 AM to 7:30 AM, an ungodly horn blows and is sure to keep anyone wide awake who is trying to sleep near the city center.

Expect Class II and III.

TROUT AND PINES

San Rafael Stream and Mike's Sky Rancho: In the high sierra of Baja a small stream tumbles and twists down from 8000 feet as invitingly as any north of the border. Thanks to a dedicated trout fisherman who decades ago hauled trout to the sparkling brook, a special breed of Baja rainbows persists where fish of any other species would be hard put to continue.

This fine little stream, which in Mexico is called a river, is reached either by working up into the mountains 50 miles from the blacktop near San Telmo south of Ensenada, or by traveling 30 miles from Valle de Trinidad over a tougher road. Each leads to the same place: Mike's Sky Rancho and Rio San Rafael.

At Mike's you are in the high sierra on the boundary of the Parque Nacional Sierra San Pedro Martir. Although the name suggests fly-in guests only, most visitors arrive by road. The accommodations are good, and a large room is $20 American whether one, two, or three people use it. Meals are family style, and you put your order in early in the day or you don't eat. The swimming pool is big, the hospitality hearty, and even when busy, hosts Mr. and Mrs. Luis Donaldson seem well supplied with friendliness and the advice of several years in Mexico.

If you want to camp at Mike's there is a meadow through which the stream runs; the charge of $5 a night includes use of the showers. There is nothing else at Mike's but the motel, the swimming pool, the bar, and the kitchen, so don't expect more when you arrive. Gasoline is not for sale at Mike's because every bit there is hauled in by pickup. Don't ask for it except in an emergency. Also, there is no fishing tackle for sale.

From the Pass at mile 19 Mile's Sky Rancho occupies a mountain meadow at 6,000 feet along San Rafael Creek.

The trout will bite on worms or flies. There is no closed season and no limit, but a license is required. Licenses are available at the border towns; or in Ensenada, at Avenida Ruiz Number 4; or by mail from the Mexican Government Fisheries Office at 395 W. 6th St., San Pedro CA 90731. They are $8 a year or $4 for three days. Since the stream has only a limited number in its short length, the wise sportsman will take only a very few of these brilliant Mexican trout. They survive in a shallow swift mountain stream that is almost everywhere narrow enough to be jumped across, and they evade coyotes, drought, disease, surging snow runoffs, and fishermen. Unlike their yankee rainbow cousins, though, these Mexican rainbows act strangely like California browns and loch levens. At the slightest sound or shadow, or footfall and vibration, they dart from their feeding spot, hide below a rock or log, and will not come out again to feed.

Only the stealthy fisherman will take these small, spunky trout, which run 8 to 10 inches in length and rarely reach 12 or more inches. They may be fished either upstream or downstream from the motel. Because the stream simply disappears into the earth several miles below the motel, the fish are totally locked into their environment, their continued life guaranteed only by summer springs and winter snows.

A fall a mile above Mike's Sky Rancho cascades the year around on San Rafael Creek. Mexican rainbows provide challenging fishing.

A road runs upstream on the south bank, then crosses to the north bank. The fishing is better above this crossing. Near here an often-photographed waterfall tumbles several feet over large granite rocks and forms a relatively large pool, absent of fish of course. Downstream there is a trail through high brush and although the altitude reduces the danger of rattlesnakes, one should always be alert and careful along this stream.

The run in from Valle de Trinidad is 30 miles and three hours over Class III with some short stretches of IV. The run in from San Telmo is 50 miles and four hours over Class II and III with some short stretches of IV. The road is paved as far south as Valle de Trinidad, and San Telmo is only 5 miles off the pavement of Mex 1.

VALLE DE TRINIDAD TO MIKE'S SKY RANCHO & MIKE'S SKY RANCHO TO SAN TELMO

MILE

This run to a pine forest and sparkling stream can be made from either direction. This log begins in Valle de Trinidad, since this route involves the least amount of dirt-road driving. It ends in San Telmo and may be reversed for a drive beginning at that end. Valle de Trinidad, reached from Ensenada via Mex 16, is the last place to fill up with gas and supplies before journeying into the mountains. Set your trip gauge at 0 at the Valle de Trinidad Pemex.

0

10.5 At this distance east and south of Valle de Trinidad the new paved road ends. A sign may point to the right, toward a barren desert; it will announce: "Mike's Sky Ranch 20 miles." This is a sharp right off the road to San Felipe. Set your trip gauge at 0 here.

0

2.2 You have gone up a long, slowly rising grade and come to a gate. Be sure to close it after passing through. This is a good road with few rocks. Vegetation is sparse and low growing.

5.0 Fork right, keep left.

6.1 Rancho road left, keep right.

7.9 Old gate, some deep sand; use caution.

8.4 Pass old rancho and begin Class III grade up. .8 up.

9.2 Top.

10.7 Begin Class III grade up. 1 mile up.

11.7 Top.

14.7 *Major Intersection:* Marked by sign, go left.

16.3 Arroyo with water, some water crossing necessary.

16.9 Ranch road right, keep straight ahead, go upgrade.

17.6 Top, view point, begin steep descent, Class III.

Leaving Mike's Sky Ranch the road winds up and away to the south. Set trip-gauge at 0 at motel.

0

3.3 Road right to Simpson's Ranch and course of Baja motorcycle race. The road here moves steeply upward with sharp dropoffs to the right and occasional views of the San Rafael River.

3.9 Road left to Mike's Sky Ranch airport.

5.2 Dropping down, road enters area of trees with corral to right. Some sand in road.

13.8 Road branches backward to the left. Keep straight ahead.

14.4 *Major Intersection:* Some signs. Either way will lead to San Telmo. The more dramatic and interesting is to the left. Go sharp left and travel south on plateau on sandy, dusty road for 5 miles.

19.2 *Major Intersection:* No signs. Main road you are on seems to angle gently around to the left and fork is backward and to the right. Left takes you to the Observatory (see page 68) and right takes you to San Telmo. A second fork is ahead.

19.4 Intersection with road to right. Keep left and head for the high saddle off to the left. Do not go right. Dead-ends.

20.3 You are on high, barren, rolling mountains of strange beauty. Road branches left, keep right.

25.6 You are high over a spectacular descent of the mountains toward the ocean. The road here can be hair-raising and on-coming traffic could present an unsolvable problem. Sheer dropoffs on the right side and steep mountainsides on the left. The road surface is fair to good with few rough spots, but it is very narrow.

29.5 You have finished the steep drop from the mountains. After going through an old riverbed that the road follows you enter a wide valley with wheat fields and ranches.

29.6 A sign reading "Parque Nacional" points to where you have come from.

30.0   **Ranch on flat plain to right. Fences begin.**

31.8   **Gate, and sign read "Observatorio" pointing the way you have come.**

32.1   **Fork in road from Buena Vista and alternate to Mike's from 14.4 reenters here.**

33.5   **Fork left. Sign says "Observatorio." Keep right. Large wheat fields and ranch.**

36.9   **Sinaloa store on left: soda pop, beer, some groceries. No gas.**

44.0   **San Telmo and improved, wider road. Gas, food, no lodging.**

49.9   **Mex 1 pavement, Ensenada 80 miles north.**

Expect Class II and III to Mike's Sky Ranch with some very short sections of IV.
Expect Class III from Mike's to San Telmo with short sections of IV and, nearing San Telmo, some I and II.

EXTRAORDINARY NATIONAL PARK

It may have been encountering snow in Baja. It may have been climbing in just a few hours from sea level to the brisk, cold air of 9,000 feet. Or it may have been the seemingly endless stands of great pine forests. Whatever it was that the 75,000 hectare* national park in the granite-rich Sierra San Pedro Martir did to us, it did it completely.

On the last day of a December expedition photographer Robert Western and myself were there, 140 miles south of Ensenada, near the towering 10,126-foot granite slab of Picacho Diablo—the highest point in Baja California—and we said to each other: "This is the perfect way to spend a final day in Baja."

Travelers go up this road never suspecting what is really there. They go to see the observatory and to casually view Baja's highest point. And in these high, hidden forests and big mountain valleys, they stumble on places they would not have believed Baja possessed.

The view from the observatory, where the cliffs drop away into the eastern desert off the massive Mexican escarpment, makes the view from Glacier Point in Yosemite seem pretty tame. And across the way the sheer bright-gray walls of Picacho Diablo's north face, glowing golden in the afternoon's final sun, sweep up to over 10,000 feet above a canyon, the floor of which remains mysteriously out of sight.

But the park's surprises don't end with the captivating mystery of Picacho Diablo or with the great forested cliffs falling away on all sides from the observatory site. The park's streams and forests are open to back-packing and trail-riding on horses supplied at Meling Ranch. Horses are available by reservation only. Write to: Meling Ranch, Box 224, Ensenada, Baja California, Mexico.

The park gets snow every winter and its high streams freeze up and behave like those of the High Sierra in Alta California. There is fishing in the park but no hunting. The prohibition is strictly enforced by ranger patrols and by an inspection for firearms at entry to the park.

There is a population of deer and mountain lion in the park but no bear or wild sheep. There are also lynx, bobcat, coyote, and other small animals familiar to California's Sierra Nevada.

The observatory at the end of the road is being rebuilt for the third time; this time a completely new structure five stories high will dwarf the two earlier buildings.

Leaving the Mex 1 blacktop 80 miles south of Ensenada, a good graded dirt road winds 62 miles to the observatory. The turnoff is marked by a sign indicating both "San Telmo" and "Observatorio." Since by Baja standards the road is uncommonly good, the run is a short three hours from the highway.

The cut-and-fill engineering in evidence on this route is so unusual on Baja's off-pavement endeavors that it becomes a rare gift on the drive in. One short, bad stretch could present some tough problems for a passenger auto: About 10 miles beyond San Telmo

---

*hectare is equal to 10,000 square meters, 100 ares, or 2.471 acres.

and 15 miles before the Meling Ranch are five miles of narrow rocky Class II and III arroyo and a narrow rocky Class II and III upgrade allowing little or no room for two vehicles to get around each other. But the Baja-one-lane problem, which is always popping up, seems always to be solved by good luck. There is no other answer, because there are several stretches of a mile or more where it is virtually impossible to fit two vehicles. But before and beyond this stretch the road is Class II, with short stretches of Class I until the last few miles before the observatory, where the road is Class II with some short turns and climbs of Class III.

At La Corona, about 10 miles from the top, is the park boundary with a closed gate and a guard. No motorcycles are allowed beyond this point. The entry fee is 12 pesos per vehicle plus 15 pesos per person. If you become captivated by the park and the peak, as we did, and stay until dark, at the gate there are tiny A-frame cabins containing bunks and mattresses on which you can roll out a sleeping bag. But remember, La Corona is at 7000 feet and these are unheated frame shelters. The charge is $1 American per bunk.

Meling Ranch is about one hour from the gate, but guests are accepted by reservation only. It is six hours to Ensenada from La Corona and four hours to San Quintin, the closest place with both motels and gasoline, though gasoline alone is available at San Telmo and the small towns of Camalu and Colonet.

There are no facilities of any kind at the mountaintop where the observatory is located. A tiny community of scientists lives in government-owned frame structures, and to the left of the final gate before the observatory is a small forestry camp. Neither place is set up to offer assistance or shelter to visitors. Nor is camping allowed in the vicinity of the observatory, because such camping might disturb the atmosphere or the work going on there. Large signs communicate

these prohibitions, as well as the prohibition against approaching the observatory without written permission from the Mexican government.

This permission is obtained by writing to the University of Mexico in Mexico City, Institute of Astronomy, Apartado 70-264. However, while construction continues through 1977, and possibly into 1978, all visiting permits have been canceled effective November 1, 1976 until further notice. Having driven 61 of the 62 miles, you are thus forced to take matters into your own hands if you want to reach the view. You have no choice but to walk beyond the intimidating signs, hoping for the best and prepared to use courtesy and common sense to avoid offending the authorities.

Western and I accomplished this, not without some fear. We expected at any moment to be arrested, but met not a single person. However, we don't recommend our method, and so, while construction is in progress, each person will have to select his own method of getting to the top with or without permission from Mexico City.

Below the peak and not within the shadow of Picacho Diablo, the many trails and meadows and mountain streams of this fine national park are waiting yet to be found, for the ranger at the gate informed us that it was a busy year when 300 people visited the park— less than one person a day! And while it is possible to explore the park on your own as a back-packer and fisherman it is advisable to first explore the mysteries of this park with the Meling Ranch expeditions.

Special note to motorcyclists: *No motorcycles are allowed beyond the gate at La Corona, ten miles from the observatory. This rule is strictly enforced. Many rumors purport to explain this rule, but the official reason is the same as for the prohibition in U.S. national parks: Motorcycles are barred because they can not only damage the natural terrain if used for off road forays but can also damage the dirt road itself.*

Motorcyclists are, however, welcome to park at the gate, if their object is to hike in on foot.

At 8,000 feet the snow in Baja begins. This patch is at mile 53 on the way to the Observatory.

TO THE NATIONAL PARK SIERRA SAN PEDRO MARTIR VIA SAN TELMO

MILE

Note: This entry is from kilometer 139 south of Ensenada, but the park may be entered also from Mike's Sky Rancho by turning left at mile 19.2 on the route *from* Mike's to San Telmo, on page 64.

0   At K 139 south of Ensenada. Have full tank of gas going in for this 125 mile round trip. Signs say San Telmo and Observatorio.

5.7   Village of San Telmo. Gasoline, but *Nova* only.

15.8   Road right to rancho and old mission site (25 miles of road, 15 miles of trail), keep left for Observatory.

17.2   *Major Intersection:* Left for northern route to Mike's Sky Rancho and Rancho Buena Vista, right for southern route to Mike's Sky Rancho and for observatory. This is the entry to the narrow, rocky arroyo and climb on one-lane road.

22.7   Out of arroyo and most of climb over but still going up. Here is one of the best views back down the valley. You are near kilometer post either 60 or 61. Almost every kilometer of the run to the observatory is marked by big white posts; this is the only road so marked in Baja.

24.2   Top and view back. Road is now better all the way to the observatory.

28.9   First left for Mike's Sky Rancho, keep straight ahead.

29.7   Second left for Mike's Sky Rancho, keep straight ahead. Both join mile 19.2 on Mike's to San Telmo route.

30.1   Right turnoff for Meling Ranch in view in bottom of valley to right. 2 miles down to ranch; use of facilities by reservation only. You now drop into Meling Ranch Valley and then begin climbing seriously from 2200 feet to the 9000-foot observatory. The granite wall ahead hides the many mountains and forests behind it.

46.7   National Park Gate at La Corona. Camping spaces available. Charge for entry: 12 pesos per vehicle, 15 pesos per person, driver included.

57.9   Large meadow, observatory in sight on ridge to left.

59.6   Road becomes narrow and steep as it winds to final gate.

61.2   Locked gate. Necessary to walk last mile. Small turnaround, small parking area.

Expect Class I and II on this run with some Class III and extremely short sections Class IV.

AN INACCESSIBLE MISSION

Mission Santa Maria de Los Angeles: Cataviña once was a lonely spring-fed arroyo distinguished by the blue shade of its palm trees and the surrounding tan, boulder-filled Desert of the Three Virgins. Now the modern El Presidente Motel and the adjoining Pemex station and trailer parador—each with its own imposing rectangular shape—overshadow the small stream of water leaving the Cataviña Oasis.

Just one mile south of this modern El Presidente complex, at an intersection well marked by a red and white mission-restoration sign, a paved fork from the main road runs the short distance to Rancho Santa Ines.

If you plan to attempt the road to Mission Santa Maria, which has one of Baja's toughest arroyo cross-

Near the oasis of Cataviña every traveler is impressed by the profusion of boulders, cirio trees, and giant cardon cactus. The author is dwarfed by this 50 foot cardon.

AN INACCESSIBLE MISSION

ings—and indeed is one of the most challenging routes available—you had better start with a cup of coffee at the Rancho Santa Ines.

The ranch is a famous stop on both the old and new Baja race courses, but no one pretends it is anything more now than a small ranch with a small unpretentious counter from which to serve an occasional tourist. The El Presidente complex does all the business, and Santa Ines is pretty quiet.

They won't tell you at Santa Ines about the bunks for rent for $2 a night (supply your own sleeping bag) or offer much information, but the food is good and the prices fair, particularly when compared to pre-devaluation prices at the El Presidente. The best example is the El Presidente's charge for a cold beer: $2.50 American; the same beer, equally cold, cost 64¢ at Ines. Since devaluation the same bottle costs $1 at the El Presidente and 35¢ at Ines.

If you state that you plan to drive to Santa Maria and ask for information about the road, the odd stares mean you have been accepted as another loco gringo. For, in the local opinion, only a person not fully sane would want to drive to that deserted hole in the mountains. The road goes nowhere; there is nothing where it ends.

A helpful ranch hand will tell you repeatedly:

"Es Camino muy malo, señor. *Muy malo!*"

You might change your mind. But if you don't, keep some things in mind about the Santa Maria road. The road *is* short, but its few really difficult parts qualify it as one real Baja-Mule-of-a-Bad-Road. Four-wheel-drive is absolutely essential. But even tough roads have some good points and the Santa Maria road is no exception.

The really bad places are at the three miles each at the beginning and the end of this 15-mile-long road. Not only are the middle nine miles a pleasure to drive and explore, but the surrounding country is filled with boulder landscapes, arroyos of white sand, and cactus and palms that make the country just plain good to look at and be in.

But don't relax. If you break down on this road chances are your vehicle will become another rusting

At the Mission Santa Maria site springs still flow in the rocky, boulder strewn valley; frogs croak, and a feeling of desolation triumphs.

Baja landmark. What goes in here is just going to have to come out under its own power.

So the road is a mixture of Baja's worst and best. And the history of the mission is equally paradoxical. Only a year after it was founded, in 1767, it was abandoned because of the worldwide expulsion, in 1768, of Jesuits from Spanish lands. And so after much back-breaking work and a successful beginning, the mission was left to decay, for it was not taken over by the Dominicans who replaced the expelled Jesuits.

AN INACCESSIBLE MISSION

From this lonely mission site east of Cataviña Junipera Serra began his journey to Alta California. Abandoned for 200 years the ruins remain standing.

At the mission site an abundant supply of water makes the hidden canyon a beautiful oasis. Frogs croak in the pools, and over the granite rocks waterfalls drop slowly from one still pool to the next. The clear water runs over sandy bottoms in defiance of the raw, hot boulder-filled mountains that so tightly enclose the little valley.

If natural beauty can steal your heart, guard it well on the road to old Santa Maria. This is a wild place but it sometimes suggests a groomed Japanese garden.

A little-known trail continues past the mission site; from the ruins it can be seen far off to the east, angling into the desolate brown hills toward Gonzaga Bay. This road is passable by vehicle for a short distance beyond the mission, but as the mountain drops off toward Gonzaga Bay, the road becomes trail. This is the original trail, the one by which the mission was founded and supplied. The road from Santa Ines was chopped out of the wilderness over a 30-year period by the owner of the ranch, who hoped to see the mission one day restored.

The road to the mission begins behind the ranch, but is not easy to find. Get someone from the ranch to point it out, otherwise you are most apt to follow the wrong road around the edge of the long airport. The correct road begins 100 feet past the cafe on pavement, but just before the airport it cuts left into an unlikely array of cactus and rock, drops steeply to a large corral behind the cafe, continues away from the ranch, and crosses the white sands of a dry riverbed.

Having penetrated the area behind the ranch, you climb a long, rough hill of sharp volcanic rock, drop through a terrible arroyo, and cross the flats to a hidden, outstanding view of the Sea of Cortez. The view is literally stunning and breathtaking.

You then drop down, and drop down more and more, wondering how you will ever get out. You then pass through a palm forest and the deep sands of the oasis and over more granite to the site.

If you don't break down or get stuck, the drive in takes three to four hours. Coming out takes a little less because you will know the road.

At the site the front and back walls of the main mission building stand intact. The outline of the building is clear. The foundations of outbuildings are still there and some rock dams and corrals are easy to find. From perennial disuse the site is clean and unlittered. Beyond the great silence broken only by the sound of water and frogs and the grandeur of the enclosing mountains, there is nothing else.

If this road and the "inaccessible mission" in the hidden valley at its end are not the best Baja has to offer, as some insist they are, they are without question high on the list.

MILE CATAVIÑA TO MISSION SANTA MARIA

0   Begin at Santa Ines corral.

.3   Cross white sands of dry river, go uphill to left.

.5   Steep rocky road, sharp volcanic rock; sometimes you must leave road and turn out into cactus to avoid washouts.

1.6   Begin down to cross stream bed. March through June will find it alive with bright blossoms or flowers. *Do not try to cross this arroyo without first walking it.* Walk it thor-

oughly, and go several hundred feet up the other side. It's the worst part of the crossing: Class VII.

2.6   Reach flats. Mountains east are sharp and clear, dramatic boulders to the right. You have fair going to mile 9.0

4.8   Twist and wind on smooth, limestone base, work into wide canyon with twin peaks to right.

5.8   Blacktop peak to left and various camping spots. Cross several riverbeds of white sand.

7.5   Leave rocks and move over plateau to last mountains. If it is morning you will be driving straight into sun.

9.0   Tough arroyo: Class V.

9.8   Top divide. Road drops steeply to left and degenerates rapidly from Class V to VI and VII. Enters narrow, steep boulder-filled canyons.

11.2   Degenerate to Class VIII and IX with some Class X and stream bed.

13.0   Mild improvement to Class VII and VIII, first view of palms and clear pools of water. Steep downgrades.

13.5   Road enters deep sand of stream bed, winds into tall shady palm trees, Class VII deep sand. After .3 mile, climb out to right. Begin over rocky narrow granite path, Class VIII.

14.5   Mission site. Spring and water 100 feet northwest. Not recommended for drinking. Road continues four miles further before ending at the steep dropoff to the old trail to Gonzaga Bay.

Expect Classes III to X on this challenging road.

BOULDER LAND

Mission San Fernando Velicata: The shortest dirt-road route to mission ruins is 38 miles south of El Rosario on Mex 1. A weathered red and white mission-restoration sign indicates the right turn.

The sign says it is 5 miles in to the mission site, but it is only 3.1. It is a Class II road in, but the last .2 of a mile is Class III, so if you are driving a low-clearance vehicle, it's best to park and walk those last steps.

A rancho neighbors the ruins. Most days its big round corral enjoys activity of some sort. On my last visit an orphaned calf was being bottle fed by two big vaqueros who were concerned lest he die also.

Although small, enough of the ruins remain to suggest what it must have been like to live in this little valley in the late eighteenth century surrounded by a thousand and more local Indians.

The only Baja mission founded by Father Junipero Serra, the Franciscan of California mission fame, it endured until 1818, when it was abandoned to the elements.

MEX 1 TO MISSION RUINS
SAN JUAN DE VELICATA

MILE	
	You will have driven south from El Rosario 38 miles, or north from Cataviña 32 miles to reach the marked turnoff. It is marked for southbound traffic only. It is 1.5 miles north of the tiny cafe and windmill at El Progreso. Set trip-gauge at 0 at turnoff.
0	
1.0	**Road forks left to El Progreso. Keep right along high road. Some rocks in road.**
1.8	**Road angles right and turns back north. Unless you have 4WD, do not attempt to take any of the left turnoffs across the riverbed to El Progreso.**
2.9	**Road deteriorates; park vehicle in turnaround and walk last .2 of a mile to ruins on low rise to right.**

3.1   **Ruins on right with mission-restoration sign. Expect Class II and, small part III.**

The Penjamo, Aguila, Agustin Ruins: In the same area as San Fernando de Velicata, a stretch of original Baja 1000 road survives. A good one-day trip will show what it was like to try to drive Baja before pavement.

After leaving Velicata the pavement continues south past El Progreso (a cafe on the highway with a dry, dusty village one mile west) at 39 miles from El Rosario, Cecelia Station at 41 miles, and the Catariña turnoff at 42.7 miles. From the Catariña turnoff it is 1.3 miles to the left turn onto the old Baja Road.

A second left turn into the same road is another mile south on Mex 1; a third well-marked turn into it, via Guayaquil, is a mile further south.

This old section of road parallels the new highway and about a mile east of it in the desert passes through old Baja 1000 stops in which past memories linger.

At Rancho Penjamo, where travelers once stopped to rest in the shade and buy soda pop, I talked with the Señora as she shaded her eyes from the sun.

"Who comes this way these days?" I asked.

"No one," she shook her head.

"No tourists, nada," I couldn't believe it.

"Never. No one," she repeated.

"Motorcycles?"

She shrugged a no.

"Do you sell cold drinks any longer?" I asked, hoping she did.

"Lo siento pero no mas." She was leaning against the ranch fence built of dead dry cactus limbs. When I asked her why, she pointed west to the highway and said all the tourists were there now, where the government wanted them.

It was the same at the other old stops. The cutoff runs 12 miles to San Agustin Parador, passing through Penjamo, Aguila, and Guayaquil. After 12 miles it is best to rejoin the pavement; the old road deteriorates badly on its way back to Mex 1, just north of Cataviña.

CUTOFF THROUGH RANCHO PENJAMO, AGUILA, GUAYAQUIL TO SAN AGUSTIN PARADOR

MILE

At 1.3 miles south of Santa Catarina turn-off there is a left turn into the desert, sometimes marked by a sign saying "Penjamo."

0 Set trip-gauge at 0 here.

.8 Level road winds in among high cactus and proceeds to the side of a rocky hill where high cardon cactus grow and then drops into a passable, Class III arroyo. Take it slowly. To the right dry stream bed meanders.

1.0 Rancho Penjamo, windmill and water, shade; no facilities.

2.5 Guayaquil, a tiny settlement with a school building, a deserted municipal building, and a small rancho that once served dusty travelers. Now you will get a friendly wave, directions, and a feeling of sadness. There are no facilities in Guayaquil. The road passes behind ranchos and into the center of the village, just as it did when it was the only main road in Baja.

4.0 Come to the ranch and store of El Aquila. A windmill pumps water and a corral holds cattle. But the store is no longer in operation. Old dry live-oak trees twist up from the desert earth. The road is Class II with some III. It runs by the porch of the ranch house. Beyond here you may encounter some deep sand.

5.5 100 yards of deep sand in two ruts. Keep left.

6.5 Keep left. The road forks often, but most branches return to each other. You are winding in a grove of trees heading generally south and you will continue to wind for about 5 miles until on the left you will make out, over the trees, the windmill of Rancho San Agustin. An airport will appear, small, gravel-surfaced. The pavement of Mex 1 is one mile hard right at San Agustin Parador. The trip to El Marmol may be started at this point. Check gas and supplies first.

Expect Class II with short stretches of III.

El Marmol from San Agustin Parador to Cataviña: This exciting offbeat trip should be taken by itself and not mixed with another. When you arrive in El Marmol you will want to poke around the old ghost town and not be rushed. And because the roads are bad, you will want all day to work your way slowly over the rocky hills and stream beds.

This is a loop trip; the path out is not the same as the one in. If you are camped around Cataviña you drive north 20 miles to the San Agustin Parador. From there the 32-mile loop into El Marmol and back out to Cataviña requires four-wheel-drive. If it were a matter of life or death, a pickup truck might complete this loop, but not without damage.

At El Marmol the several abandoned buildings include a schoolhouse of pure onyx; there are also a cemetery and the onyx mine. Huge blocks of quarried onyx are stacked in great piles, readied for shipment long ago. Until the late 1950s this mine supplied almost the entire world demand for the onyx used in pen and pencil desk sets. From here the big blocks of lowgrade marble were trucked to Catarina Landing and shipped to Ensenada. With the coming of plastics both the mine and the town have died.

If you have the right vehicle, El Marmol is well worth exploring. And if you don't want to make the loop, two-wheel-drive, high-clearance truck can come out the same way it went in. The roughest part of the road is beyond El Marmol.

The two parts of the trip are also different in their landscape. The first part, going in, is over relatively barren rocky desert, while the second part, beyond El Marmol, going out, winds through the Las Tres Virgenes Desert of big boulders and low, steep rocky ridges. Toward the end it becomes, after the spring

The lonely graveyard at El Marmol is a short walk from the abandoned town site. The flowers of this wire wreath are long departed.

rains, a rock garden with parklike places—greenery, yellow blossoms, tall cardon cactus, and thick stands of curling, leaning boojum trees.

For an overnight trip El Marmol offers a good spot to camp, though there is no water or anything else. You have to be self-sufficient. The land is level and clean.

EL MARMOL & BEYOND VIA
MILE SAN AGUSTIN & BACK TO CATAVIÑA

0 At the San Agustin Parador there is a Pemex station and some groceries. Set your trip-gauge at 0 here. The turn is past the Highway Department building up toward the water tower, straight east into the desert.

.7 You have gone over the hill away from the parador toward Rancho San Agustin and will cross the airport and low, dry riverbed; through a grove of trees and up to the rancho.

1.2 Rancho Agustin, old Baja stop; no services now of any kind, nothing but directions. Corral of dried cardon cactus, old

California Automobile Association triangular sign c. 1945.

4.6 *Major Intersection*: At San Agustin drive straight into the barren desert across flats with various forking routes which all go southeast. At this intersection, about 3.5 miles south of San Agustin, you join the road in from Rancho Sonora on Mex 1. This is an alternate route to El Marmol. The stretch between San Agustin and here is over volcanic rock and often in a stream bed. 4WD is necessary. Class III and IV sometimes winding into the desert to avoid serious erosion in the stream bed road. Here the road improves after joining the Rancho Sonora Road, and continues toward El Marmol.

8.0 After traveling 3.4 miles on the improved section of road you will reach a windmill on the right, abandoned along an old, dry arroyo. Road begins to get rougher. Class III and IV with some V. Road starts to climb toward El Marmol in the hills.

9.7 Airport hill on left. Road is winding up to El Marmol.

11.4 Arrive at site of mine and town. Here you will decide whether to return the way you came in or to continue over the hills to Cataviña, about 21 miles of rough desert road. If you do, the road is hard to find. The only clue is visible to the right, above the onyx quarry. There you see road cuts in the hill, for the road out of El Marmol exits west over the big hill, switchbacking up the big rocks. (Don't follow the road south out of El Marmol; it ends in cactus and sand a few hundred yards into the mountain.) The hill and the rough, rocky switchback beyond, are a major hurdle. If you can do it, the rest is possible. On the other side there is an equally steep descent over huge rock slabs that can make little claim to being roadway. This is Class VII and VIII road.

22.0 You have gone over 11 long lonely miles of little-used 4WD pathway, twisting and turning, often wondering where you are, but winding most often west-southwest through large boulders, down into little stream beds, over steep ridges, and back down again with never a sign of another vehicle or of man or beast. This is not a really bad road here, but on it you are alone. These 11 miles are Class IV and V.

23.0 *Major Intersection*: Here join old Baja 1000 road. It comes in on a curve from the right, and as you join it you angle left or straight ahead down it. Many old race signs will begin to appear on the rocks.

24.1 Shrine on right. Road surface improves to Class II and III.

24.9 Shrine on left and old home of man who for years maintained this shrine and sold soft drinks when this was the main road. Now it is deserted. A picture of the virgin remains on the rocks.

31.6 Road forks to right, keep left.

32.1 Arrive at blacktop of Mex 1, a reassuring sight in this maze of roads and rolling, boulder-filled hills. You are 2.4 miles north of the parador at Cataviña.

Expect Classes III and IV going in with some VI.

Expect Classes V and VI going out of El Marmol south, with VII and VIII in the beginning and II and III at the end.

THREE OLD MINING TOWNS

El Arco: In 1920 the center of a gold-mining effort in the nearby mountains, El Arco is spread about on rocky land, much like Virginia City, Nevada.

It is a total of 40 miles of paved road from Guerrero Negro: 15 miles on Mex 1 to the cutoff, then 26 miles on an unnumbered Mexican highway to the tiny gathering of buildings, where about 200 persons live.

In El Arco there are a small military camp, a grocery, two cafes, and a scattering of old buildings worth examining for their historical curiosity and photographic appeal. Gasoline and food can be purchased at the little tree-shaded yellow-front grocery adjacent to the paved highway.

At El Arco the pavement ends. The town, spread about on both sides of a wide, deep arroyo, is not compact. In fact, so thoroughly is it scattered there is no feeling of a town at all. But this is a supply point for several interior areas and several roads lead from it to the mountains.

Lodging is not available, and most people secure their supplies in Guerrero Negro before coming here or passing through to the interior.

MILE **GUERRERO NEGRO TO EL ARCO**

0 Set trip-gauge at 0 at the northern Pemex—not the one by the big eagle, but the one at the bend in town. Drive straight east out of town to the big Y and go right, south down Mex 1 for 20 miles.

20.0 Left turn at intersection marked by sign. Paved road proceeds east through flat Vizcaino desert and then enters mountains.

24.0 Enter foothills and wind toward El Arco.

26.5 Enter El Arco. Barren, deserted-looking gathering of small buildings and tiny dwellings. Cafe alone on left, blue and white, sometimes open. Cross deep arroyo. Old church on right, other old buildings. On left grocery with gasoline. Road makes sharp bend to right and pavement ends.

Pozo Aleman: "German Village," beyond El Arco, though smaller, more compact, and virtually uninhabited (only a man and his daughter now live

Near El Arco the old mining town of Pozo Aleman, "German Village," retains many old structures but only three inhabitants.

there), is far more interesting than El Arco. In Pozo Aleman the feeling of the gold-mining effort is kept alive by the old rusting equipment, the vice on the homemade bench coming out of a twisted, dead tree trunk, the adobe buildings on the skyline, the old windmill and winding road. Several of its old, deserted buildings remain in good condition.

In the maze of roads leaving El Arco, the exact path of the two-mile trip to Pozo Aleman is difficult to find. The road in is Class II with sections of III.

MILE	EL ARCO TO POZO ALEMAN
0	Set trip-gauge at 0 in El Arco at the sharp bend in road just before pavement ends. Go straight through town instead of making the right turn on pavement and this will bring you to a steep drop into the arroyo. Cross this and keep to the right.
1.0	Road drops into rocky area similar to stream bed and narrows. It follows this old stream bed right into Pozo Aleman.
2.0	Enter Pozo Aleman. Dwelling on left, large building on horizon, warehouse to right. Park ahead on right. If you have gone fur-

ther than 2.5 miles you had better turn back and try again to find the right road to Pozo Aleman. An aid in finding this road is to seek the road to El Barril or San Francisquito, since that is the road that passes through Pozo Aleman.

Expect Class II and III.

Las Flores: Very little is left of this old silver-mining site, but it remains attractive. It is 10 miles south of easily reached Bahia de Los Angeles (420 paved miles south of Tijuana) on a dirt and sand Class II road.

To your right heading out are high mountains populated by mountain sheep; to your left is the beautiful bay. At the site an old donkey engine, some adobe walls, and some dangerous shafts remain. Higher in the hills are other portions of the old tramway, but these should not be attempted without a guide.

Antero Diaz, who is Mr. Bahia de Los Angeles by virtue of his long pioneering effort on the harsh shores, is the man to contact. In a graveyard just behind the old site is buried Dick Daggett, an English sailor who was a Baja pioneer.

BAHIA DE LOS ANGELES
TO LAS FLORES
MILE

0   In Bahia de Los Angeles set your trip-gauge at 0 at the Pemex station just across from the motel of Antero Diaz. Go by the motel and out of town toward the dumps, south just above the shore of the bay. The road will turn inland, wind into the low foothills, pass the dumps and its vultures, and move back down toward the southern salt flats of the bay.

5.1   Road forks left for southern lagoon of bay, keep right for Las Flores. The road will deteriorate slightly here and the sand is deep, but it passable in a carefully driven two-wheel-drive vehicle. Watch for big holes.

9.9   **Arrive Las Flores ruins. Time in route: 40 minutes.**

Expect Class II.

VIZCAINO

Vizcaino: The side road just beyond a large Pemex station leads to one of Mexico's more interesting farming experiments. In what was believed to have been an impossible place to grow any kind of crops, the government has set up an experimental farm.

By use of water from wells drilled deep in the sandy desert, the cultivation of various herbs and crops and trees is attempted, and scientists and horiculturists from many countries around the world keep track of what is going on in Vizcaino. The small town, with perhaps 500 people, is placed neatly on the desert with regular city blocks, a town square, a municipal building, a church, and warehouses. All around it are neat, well-tended fields and orchards.

It is five miles of pavement in and five miles back out. There is gas at the Pemex station on Mex 1 just above the turnoff, and there is food at the grocery in Vizcaino but no lodging. This is not a tourist town, but the variety of flowers growing, the way the town is kept up, the people busy in the fields make this short trip worthwhile. No road-log is needed.

CLOSE-BY BACK COUNTRY

Santa Agueda: Three miles south of the vital mining center of Santa Rosalia (see page 113) is the turnoff to Santa Agueda, a small village from which Santa Rosalia gains its water. A morning's drive in, on eleven miles of Class II and III road, will reveal a quiet town quite different from its big neighbor to the north.

There is a grocery in Santa Agueda but no cafe or motel. The main street is shaded by the same giant "India" trees that grow around the square in San

Santa Agueda is the site of Santa Rosalia's water supply and the site of the original copper strike.

Ignacio and a recent government project has created a new water system there.

Most of the way in, the old water line to Santa Rosalia is in view. The road continues on past Santa Agueda to Candeleria, a famous jumping-off spot for exploration of some of Baja's important cave paintings (see page 83).

MILE   SANTA ROSALIA TO SANTA AGUEDA

0   Set your trip-gauge at 0 at the Pemex station on the highway out of Santa Rosalia just opposite the ferry docks.

2.9   Right turn, sometimes marked by a sign. A gravel pit and an old tower are visible inland. Follow this road toward the tower.

0   Set your trip-gauge at 0 at the turnoff.

.5   Fork to right. Keep right. Class II with some III.

4.4   Rancho on left.

6.0   Enter dry arroyo, old water pipe visible; cattle here may well challenge your right of way.

7.0   Begin climb out of arroyo and up steep hill. Class III with small section IV.

8.2   Village and spring, monument.

           Expect Class II and III with some IV on grades.

San José de Magdalena: Twenty-one miles south of Santa Rosalia Mex 1 turns right into a striking river valley and runs 10 miles into the mountains to the well-kept, compact village of San José de Magdalena.

The village sits on a high plateau overlooking the sometimes running river; its small fields and gardens are neatly kept below well-built rock walls.

There is an outdoor cafe and a grocery but no gas or lodging. The drive in is over Class II and III road. Just west of town is the most dramatic cemetery in Baja.

SANTA ROSALIA TO
MILE   SAN JOSÉ DE MAGDALENA

0   Set trip-gauge at 0 at Pemex station in Santa Rosalia opposite ferry dock. Proceed 21 miles south on Mex 1.

21.0
0   Road right into mountains. No sign. Class II with some IV. Set gauge at 0.

4.4   Abandoned rancho on right. Fork left, over big round rocks, leads to active rancho and ruins of a mission site. Keep straight. Do not attempt fork left without 4WD.

9.4   Enter village of San José de Magdalena. The road continues on into the mountains to meet trails and dead-ends at Rancho Sebastian.

           Expect Class II and III with some IV.

San Bruno: The turnoff for this area, twelve miles south of Santa Rosalia, heads left toward the sea, circumventing a small military encampment. This firm sandy road loops back to Mex 1 16 miles later. It offers good access to rarely-visited Sea of Cortez beaches.

There is no gas, food, or lodging along this road. Do not take the Punta Chivato turnoff. That once modern resort has been boarded-up and is protected by a guard.

MILE   **SAN BRUNO TO MEX 1 LOOP**

0   Set trip gauge at 0 at Pemex station in Santa Rosalia opposite ferry docks.

12.0 Left turn off Mex 1 for San Bruno dirt road along beach.

0   Set trip gauge at 0.

4.5   Left turn to beach. Old fishing camp. Rocky, some sand, fair parking. Possible to camp. Water clean and gentle. Old fish bones about.

8.2   Arrive at the brick structure of Rancho San Marco.

9.3   Cross arroyo and continue to Ejido San Bruno where there is a school, a ranch, and, some days, cowboys working cattle.

10.4 Rancho El Mezical. Work west and to right to get back to highway. Road winds through cactus. Fair surface. Class II and III all the way.

16.5 Reach Mex 1 pavement and large sign indicating Punta Chivato turnoff.

La Candelaria and the cave paintings: Hidden in the high mountain canyons north and south of San Ignacio are examples of Baja's ultimate mystery, and perhaps its outstanding treasure: the many beautiful red and yellow cave paintings of deer, sheep, fish, rabbits, and human figures.

In *The Cave Paintings of Baja California*, explorer-writer Harry Crosby has put together an exciting, definitive, written and pictorial account of the cave paintings that he has been able to locate and photograph.

The cave painters looked out over this valley and perhaps their paintings were an effort to dominate its vastness.

The site that awakened his interest in the ancient painters' work can be reached by road. The paintings there are on a huge white boulder that overlooks a wide, serene valley in the high Sierra Guadalupe Mountains, south of San Ignacio and west of Santa Rosalia.

The boulder, having fallen from the mountaintop now rests halfway down its slope, facing the valley and creating a place for prehistoric hunters to rest and gain shelter from the elements. It also presented a protected surface on which to paint. And on it were painted the stunning red profiles of an antlered deer and a sheep with curling horns as well as other minor figures that have become badly weathered with age.

Crosby does not include a picture of this group of paintings in his book, because, to hazard a guess, they are probably the least represenatative. If this is

It's 30, long, rocky miles from Mex 1 to the rock art near Rancho La Candelaria.

so, the other paintings must be overwhelming. For the group at La Candelaria is infectious, and once seen the mind is turned, as was Crosby's, to constant wonder: Who created this beautiful art? When? Why? None of these questions is even now close to being answered. As far back as the sixteenth century, the indigenous people of the Baja Peninsula could not tell Cortez where the paintings had come from or who the painters had been.

It takes almost all day to drive the 30 miles over one of Baja's rockier routes to Rancho Candelaria via Santa Agueda, so plan on camping overnight somewhere before the ranch and taking several hours the next morning to walk in and examine and photograph the site.

Someone from the rancho will have to guide you. From the ranch it is a 45-minute walk along cattle trails winding through a dusty, cactus-lined track, then left, up over a little ridge and along the slope of an adjoining ridge to where the boulder sits facing east and south. We paid our guide 50 pesos.

Like other ranches in the valley west of Santa Agueda, this rancho is run by the Villavicencios. The elder Villavicencio at Candelaria, who is unmarried, cares for his sister and two tall, deaf-mute brothers. The Baja Villavicencios are descended from a tall Spanish soldier who landed with the Jesuits. Most are over six feet tall, and the deaf-mute who guided us to the paintings was no exception.

It is 30 miles and five hours in to Rancho Candelaria, and at least another two hours to get to and from the paintings. The road in is Class III and IV beyond Santa Agueda with some short stretches of V, but the ranchers drive in and out daily in their pickups and two-ton flatbeds.

The constant rattling is what takes its toll on this road, not the grades or road condition. The endless succession of round rocks filling the road can be maddening.

Rancho La Candelaria was settled in the nineteenth century and still uses the same well and adobe oven built many years ago.

There are several places to camp between the ranchos, but no facilities on the way, so carry all you need with you. And because you are climbing 30 miles into the mountains, by the time you get near Candelaria the nights will be cool—cold in the winter.

There is a spring and an orange grove at Candelaria. The Villavicencios are kind and patient ranchers, but while they may offer the traveler coffee or water or oranges or a guide to the paintings, they are in no other way prepared to meet or deal with tourists. But those paintings are worth every rattle and jolt to the rancho and the hot walk over the hill—and would continue to be worthwhile at twice the distance.

SANTA AGUEDA TO
MILE   LA CANDELARIA CAVE PAINTINGS

0   **At Santa Agueda. Go through town, beneath big shady trees, left at end of main street, one block uphill toward spring then right out of town and down into arroyo. You will be heading west into mountains.**

1.8   **Cross stream, road right to rancho, keep straight.**

2.0   **Class IV up.**

3.2   **Cross arroyo, large pool of water hidden to right on hairpin turn left.**

4.4   **Rock walls right and left.**

4.5   **Rancho El Bule, old foundations, huts right and left.**

8.5   **Rancho San Javier to right.**

11.8   **Rancho Tajo to right.**

13.1   *Major Intersection*: **Go right. If you are camping, this is a good area to spend the night between ranches.**

16.1   *Major Intersection:* **You are at Rancho Santa Rosa. The road you have been on continues straight ahead to Rancho Rincon. From a windmill on your right a plastic line spans overhead to the rancho on the left. Just**

ahead, past the corral, there is a dim track leading to the right from the road you are on. This is the way to Rancho Candelaria. If you are at all confused, get directions from the rancher. If camping, the area between Santa Rosa and Candelaria is also suitable for an overnight stay. Camp away from the ranchos to avoid barking dogs, cattle, and chickens.

19.8   After taking right fork at Santa Rosa you reach Rancho Candelaria directly below the high peaks of a large mountain. The road terminates at a rock corral in front of the ranch house. You may ask here about the caves. However, since the site is technically less a cave than a boulder with paintings on its outer face, ask about the "pinturas" and you may be better understood.

Expect Class III and IV from Santa Agueda to Candelaria.

A HIDDEN CITY

La Purisima and San Isidro: Stories are often heard of the mountain oases and their protecting canyons, but few tourists actually see these places. In two trips to the Comondus, Purisima, and Javier as late as 1976 I never saw another tourist, or even another tourist vehicle on the hundreds of miles of mountain roads entering and leaving these three, green, hidden retreats.

The Jesuit missionaries first ventured into the forbidding Sierra de la Giganta in the early eighteenth century. The present roads follow their original trails just as they in turn followed the Indians.

Thus the roads to all three mountain areas are difficult, and if passible in a four-wheel drive vehicle, they present quite a driving challenge to a two-wheel-drive pickup. A truck with a camper on back will encounter tough going, with or without four-wheel-drive. As always, it is the few bad spots—the one or two very steep, slippery rocky grades—that make the road bad. So don't let mild entrances fool you. Going in here with a camper is possible, but could be a mistake. I particularly discourage it for campers on two-wheel-drive trucks. True, you will see Mexican passenger autos in these towns, but the American who attempts to duplicate that feat with his own passenger car can expect to abandon it somewhere along the way. If one rocky, stream-bed crossing doesn't do it, the next one will.

There *is* one way to reach these places in two-wheel-drive: Drive to Villa Insurgentes and go north up the west-coast dirt road toward San Juanico and San Ignacio, then take the turns into the mountains. But you will have to return the same way to avoid the steep mountain roads that prevent entry from the east. Because the trips described here are eastern entries over the rough road, just reverse the road logs to use the western entry.

La Purisima and San Isidro are the northernmost of the three oasis valleys. The road to Purisima offers one of the most rewarding ridge-top sights in all of Baja. After struggling long and hard with 35 miles of desert mountain road, narrow canyons, dust and dirt, you laboriously gain the final ridge and see the distant green valley revealed.

Nestled between high cliffs carved by the Purisima River, the green valley is surrounded by desert and dry, hostile mesas. In the center, not far from the lake formed by the damming of the river, is the imposing shape of El Pilon which looks like a young volcano or a great pyramid but is actually the remnant of an old mesa.

If nothing else has made it clear why the drive back out would be tortuous, the steep drop here explains well why few want to leave La Purisima to the east. On the right the rocky river is far below, at the bottom of a sheer drop. There are two small turnouts to stop and look.

Going down this steep, twisting grade with its loose rock and hairpin turns, be on the alert at all times for the trucks that boil up the terrible grade in Mexican fashion: fast and giving ground to no one. It

A HIDDEN CITY

Once on the main route down Baja this former mission site of La Purisima, an emerald oasis, is now off the beaten path.

is anyone's guess how these two- and three-ton flat-bed and stake-bed supply trucks make it in and out month after month. Probably a combination of faith, skill, daring, and an ability to repair on the road almost anything that breaks.

Like a gateway to the valley, a series of tall yellow rocks narrows the entrance; on top of them is the tiny hot village of El Arriba. Here the flume begins that parallels the road to the larger village. Its leaking makes the road muddy. Beyond the gateway of yel- low boulders, green fields suddenly appear on both sides of the road, tall trees shade the lane, and old wooden fences lean against their wires, defining the edges of various properties.

The valley is four miles long and a half-mile wide. San Isidro, the first town in the valley, sits on a dusty plateau above the fields and river, open to the sun and blazing heat, crumbling mesa slides behind it. There is a motel, a grocery, a cafe, and a tiny municipal plaza. A thousand people live and work here. Most gain entry from the west-coast road.

Slightly larger than La Purisima, San Isidro makes a good base from which to visit the mission ruins near Purisima, and the fields and the river.

Out of San Isidro the road drops again into the valley and the shade of big trees. Parallel to the narrow lane irrigation ditches bubble with clear, cold water for the tall orange trees and well-tended vineyards.

A modern white and blue school that serves both towns sits snugly in the shade in the center of the valley. If you are stared at by the brightly garbed children crowding the playing field, it's because you are quite a curiosity—a gringo a long way from the blacktop. They might shout and giggle to get your attention, and if you halt they will want to hear the strange American accent of your Spanish or the comical sounds they associate with spoken English.

In most villages their chant is similar:

"Donde va, Señor?"

And you will answer, "La Purisima."

"Porque?" they will demand.

"Tourista," you answer.

And the solemn questioning will continue as long as your Spanish or patience continues. For, unlike their parents, the children will not contain their curiosity about strangers. They will hound you on any pretext—which is not bad: It allows you one way to interact. If you halt long enough a parent may sometimes appear, and parents, too, once a contact is made, have their own array of questions about your vehicle, where you are from, and what work in the Estados Unidos you do.

When you reach any mountain village, be ready to become an instant attraction. It will pass, but in the first moments be ready to halt the children from climbing all over your equipment and you, for they will push you just as far as you let them. You will be examined, tested. But a harsh tone and direct order is easy to understand in any language, and, as in any country, it is sometimes necessary to draw a line with children.

Beyond the valley is La Purisima, a long, narrow, apparently decaying village. The road climbs out of the valley to La Purisima and the mesa where, again in the sun, there is a small grocery, some homes, the palacio municipal on the left, and the plaza on the right.

The gas station in La Purisima is at the far end of town. With many of its old buildings empty, La Purisima has a deserted air. Still, there are over 2000 people in the valley and it is well worth the drive in to discover what life is like around this desert oasis.

Camping is possible, and San Isidro has a motel and grocery as well as two cafes. In La Purisima there are other services, including a hardware store and butcher shop.

It is 40 miles and five to six hours into this valley from Mex 1 south of Mulege and the same back out. But only four-wheel-drive vehicles will get back out the same way they went in. Once in La Purisima, you have a choice of five different ways to leave. You may exit the way you entered. Or you can drive north 125 miles over dirt on the alternate truckers' route to San Ignacio, a difficult and arduous route. But one of the three final options is probably best: (1) Drive 31 miles south from La Purisima to the Comundus junction, then 64 miles back over the mountains to Mex 1. (2) Drive 61 miles south from La Purisima to the Javier junction, then 66 miles back over the mountains to Mex 1. (3) Drive 78 miles south from La Purisima to Villa Insurgentes and blacktop; *no mountains involved.*

If, like most, you choose the last, least difficult route out of La Purisima, you might wish to drive the additional 16 miles beyond Villa Insurgentes to Ciudad Constitucion, where the selection of food and lodging is far greater.

The turnoff for La Purisima (which is also the turnoff for the Comondus; see page 88) is 52 miles south of Mulege and 35 miles north of Loreto on Mex 1 at a small, lonely white cafe and dwelling called Ascencion. There is a sign.

At the cafe Feliciano Real and Señora Real will prepare a meal and offer respite from the highway before you turn in to tackle the Sierra de la Giganta. And if Feliciano has kept the cranky gas refrigerator running there will be cold drinks. Perhaps there will also be a story about the mountains.

A rider in from a nearby rancho halts at the grocery in Mulege for supplies and leaves his horse in the street.

88

THE INTERIOR

The Reals are restoring an old buckboard, grow bright pink oleanders, and care for their plot of desert land as carefully as any homeowner in an Alta California subdivision.

Each dawn Mrs. Real sweeps their square of desert sand and Feliciano carefully waters and prunes the vines and fruit trees. Their children have departed for the large cities of Mexico.

You can watch the tortillas come hot from an adobe oven fueled by desert sticks. First they are patted by Señora Real, then cooked on the oven, then dropped hot on your plate by her deft hand.

MULEGE OR LORETO
TO LA PURISIMA AND OUT
MILE

Drive 52 miles south of Mulege or 35 miles north of Loreto to Ascencion cafe. Here is the turnoff west into the mountains to both La Purisima and the Commundus. At the

0 **cafe set your trip-gauge at 0.**

3.7 **Four-way crossroads. Go sharp left. Straight ahead is ranch and windmill. Right goes 3.6 miles back to blacktop and Rancho Rosarito. Road so far is Class II and III.**

7.9 **Rancho right, begin climb up steep, very narrow grade. Class IV and V. One mile up.**

8.⁊ **Rancho right. Grade ends. Rocky arroyo crossing ahead. These are big rocks, be careful. Sometimes the road is *only* rocks.**

11.3 ***Major Intersection:* Road angles left for the Comundus, keep right and straight ahead for La Purisima. No sign.**

13.3 **Road comes in from Comundus road, keep straight ahead.**

15.0 **Road right goes to new flood-control dam. One mile to low dam. Class II and III road in. This point is at a stream crossing with high rocky cliff to right.**

16.0 **Rancho Corral de Dos Puertos is on the road to the right. Saddles rest on railings of**

desert wood and a chair and shade are offered to the weary traveler.

24.1 **Rock monument at top of grade you will proceed down. Watch for fox and coyote in this desolate section. Stay on main road. Various branches leave and return, but some don't come back. From time to time main road will narrow and deteriorate and seem to indicate that somewhere a mistake was made, a wrong turn taken, but don't worry, stay on it. This is Class III and IV on the level with Class V and VI grades and rare stretches of VII. The cactus is even and undramatic, the country rolling and seemingly endless.**

34.6 **After 10.5 miles of tough driving, sometimes not even sure of where you are, you have reached the rewarding view of the lake and green valley and the towering El Pilon. Go downhill carefully. The river crossings are no problem.**

40.0 **Village and entrance to valley. Flume comes in from left.**

42.0 **Shady, tree-lined, narrow dirt road opens on to barren, hot town of San Isidro.**

43.0 **School surrounded by shade trees and green fields.**

44.5 **La Purisima. Gas at far end of town at *Canada* sign.**

45.0 **Gas station is on right just before mile 45. Leave fertile valley and cooling shade, winding to the left toward the Pacific Ocean.**

MILE

0 **At La Purisima gas station. Here you can buy meat and groceries.**

4.9 **Jct. with coast highway. Go to right for San Ignacio. For southern points go left and up hill.**

6.7   Airstrip at top of hill bordered by painted white rocks.

8.7   Steep downgrade. Good view of surrounding coastal land. Ocean several miles to the right.

12.3   Break in mesa, a gateway through the mountains.

17.4   Ejido San Isidro. Drop off plateau on to great barren plain with straight road.

21.0   Rancho "Tres Marias" half-mile to left with windmill.

21.8   Main road angles left into hills. Straight road goes to sea.

31.2   After climbing up a series of hills you will drop down and begin to head south again. At this important and difficult to find junction the road will go off to the left like a railroad switch, right back the way you were coming. A sign for northbound traffic reads: *Camino a Cargo de la Huta Local de Caminos.* That is the elusive road to the Comondus. You will know it is the correct road by traveling down it 3 miles to a tiny homemade green sign that reads *Guatamote 2½ K.* (See page 92.)

33.0   After leaving the Comondus reverse cutoff you proceed on a narrow winding road to a junction with a new highway under construction at about mile 33. Just get on it and follow it straight south to Ejido Pancho Villa at mile 35. From Pancho Villa travel south to Pozo Grande.

41.2   Pozo Grande. Road right goes to San Jorge on the Pacific beach. Road ahead and down drops into Pozo Grande. You can purchase gasoline here from 55-gallon drums. Ask directions. There is no gasoline for sale at Pancho Villa. In Pozo Grande the road leaves the town east through the city dump and travels two miles to the new road that goes south to Villa Insurgentes. Make a sharp right at the wide graded road. For several miles this hardpacked road is fast and easy to travel. But about 10 miles south, where sand and gravel have been added to improve it, washboard suddenly begins, becoming severe enough to be dubbed the worst in all Baja. For over 30 unendurable miles, right to Villa Insurgentes, it continues without letup.

78.9   Arrive at the blacktop and Villa Insurgentes after passing almost 40 miles of irrigated fields of cotton, lettuce, onion, and other truck crops. This valley could be the San Joaquin or the Salinas in California.

Expect Class II to VI going in with some VII.

Expect Class II to III going out to Villa Insurgentes.

TWIN SHANGRI-LAS

The Comondus: Like La Purisima and San Isidro to the north, these twin villages sit in the center of the Sierra de la Giganta near a spring-fed oasis in otherwise hostile desert mountains. But unlike those larger towns to the north, these two are closer together on the bottom of their smaller valley, resting in groves of trees beside a stream.

If the easier entry from the west is used, the first town entered is San Miguel de Comondu, whose 500 people enjoy a main plaza, stores and groceries, telegraph and telephone service. Lodging is available. The gas station is ahead, in San José de Comondu.

The little valley, only four miles long and a half-mile wide, is enclosed on both sides by high cliffs, which close it in more than some would prefer. But when entered from the east, after a dry desert crossing, the lushness of the rich valley below is another of Baja's powerful desert displays.

This important junction is at mile 99 coming north from Loreto and San Javier and at mile 76.2 coming south from La Purisima. It is a "switchback" intersection. The right fork at this view (going north) goes to the Comondus and the left to the coast and La Purisima and San Ignacio.

Three miles beyond San Miguel, at the far end of the valley, on a narrow road twisting among tall shady trees past vineyards and orchards, stands the village of San José. Although both towns have the same size population, San José differs from San Miguel in consisting of one long main street lined by stores on both sides. The main road cuts left just before entering. Just beyond the town, the road winds up into the desert and off toward the east coast.

Once a few years ago, entering town on a motorcycle, I accidentally startled some cattle being herded by a man on horseback. The cattle ran off in groups of four and five, all 15 of them stampeding down the main street, their hooves clattering over the cobblestones. With equal speed, and with startling precision, the horseman sped after them, his lariat swinging and ready. Within 15 minutes he had brought back every stray steer without betraying a shadow of effort or anger. He was the picture of Mexican macho and skill in his control of the horse and the situation.

On a quiet Sunday last year, I stopped to rest in front of the new government building between San Miguel and San José. From the building emerged a young man dressed in slacks, shirt and tie. I took him for a recent college graduate, probably a village teacher. We said hello and talked for a few minutes. He was a doctor from outside the village. Although obviously young, his quick, incisive replies and questions marked him as alert and educated, with a sensitive concern for his work and for the village.

He had returned that day to check on a woman whose child he had delivered by caesarean section the week before.

We talked in Spanish about the Comondus, and though we both agreed on their natural beauty and tranquillity I was surprised when he said, "But of course they are dying. They will not be here in ten years."

Asked why, he said, "The young people do not wish to stay and work. They want to go to the big cities. These mountain places are left with the old people only."

"But won't the young people be disappointed by life in the big cities and return here to make their lives?"

"Why should they? As Mexicans their life will be better in the cities. They don't want to work the earth the way their fathers do here."

"Do you see a change in this trend?"

"No."

"But it is so peaceful here, so tranquil. How can they want to go somewhere else?"

"They want to live in the cities. They don't want what is here. Is it not the same in America?"

"To an extent, but people in America are beginning to rediscover the pleasures of rural living."

"Here it is not that way. In Mexico we are still leaving the country, and before we learn to come back places like this will die."

We parted and I drove up to San José, sobered by the thought of no one living any longer in this place. I wondered if the young doctor was correct. I feared he was.

San Miguel came into being about 1715, when the famous Father Ugarte, a Jesuit missionary, started a visiting station there. He hauled in thousands of

On the road out of the Comondus many ranchos line the route and a chance to compare modes of transportation over coffee is good. This black burro sports a fine saddle of famous "Miraflores Leather" from Baja California Sur while the red Honda utilizes a modern foam cushion.

mule-loads of earth to improve and enlarge the areas suitable for cultivation, and for trees. Later the visiting site was to receive full status as a mission. In San José there was also an early mission, a portion of which has been saved and is being restored.

By the difficult eastern entry, it is 40 miles to the Comondus from Mex 1 at Ascencion; by the much easier western entry, it is 70 miles to the Comondus from Villa Insurgentes. All services, *though none are tourist-oriented*, are available.

Unlike the La Purisima–San Isidro log, the following log has been written from the western side and for two-wheel-drive. If you are in four-wheel-drive and want to tackle the eastern route exit, the log continues out to Mex 1 to offer a loop. If you use two-wheel-drive to either La Purisima or the Comondus be sure to return the way you came: by the western route. Do not attempt the 40 miles out of either place over the Sierra de la Giganta; if you do, you will ruin your equipment. When you've seen the valleys you've seen the best. If tough roads are your desire, then come back and make the whole loop with four-wheel-drive or a motorcycle.

VILLA INSURGENTES TO THE COMONDUS AND EASTERN EXIT TO ASCENCION

MILE

0 Set trip-gauge at 0 at the big Pemex station on the west side of the main street in Villa Insurgentes. Begin north out of town on the pavement, which ends at the edge of town. Keep going north on this wide, graded Class I road toward Santo Domingo and Pozo Grande.

18.4 Right turn to Mission San Javier road over the mountains to Sea of Cortez and Loreto, 66 miles. Sign says only *Camino a Cargo de la Huta Local de Caminos*. The fields here are fenced. The road to the Comondus continues on past this turnoff. Keep going north.

35.9 *Major Intersection:* Turn left here for Pozo Grande. Straight goes to El Crucero, a rancho. It is 2 miles left to the town. The entry is disappointing, through the dumps. But gas is available from 55-gallon drums if you forgot to get it in Villa Insurgentes. No lodging or food.

37.9 Leave Pozo Grande north for Ejido Pancho Villa.

40.9 Ejido Pancho Villa, a desolate, flat gathering of huts. No gas, food, or lodging.

44.4 Construction begins. Use the new wide dirt highway to continue north, but be careful: The left-hand exit onto the old road must be taken. The new road north, on its way to the Comundus road, simply ends in the desert, but before it ends it turns to deep sand ready to mire down if not swallow a 2-wheel-drive.

47.8 Here the construction splits; the old road winds off north paralleling for a short distance the new road, which gradually disappears to the northeast. The old road, Class II and III, reaches the coast, but before it does you turn right to the Comondus. These are low, sandy hills, with low cactus and brush: typical Pacific coast vegetation.

51.4 *Major Intersection:* Here you are at the barely discernible western entry road into the Comondus. The only sign is the worn, rusted government announcement: *Camino a Cargo de la Huta Local de Caminos*. Approached from the south, this intersection is like a Y; take the right fork, the one that goes nearly straight ahead. The left fork goes almost straight, then left, and, in a few miles, sharper left for the coast and the run north. For greater accuracy, reset trip-gauge at 0 at this intersection.

0 At right turnoff.

2.7 Green sign on right says "Guatamote 7 kms." Keep straight ahead.

7.9 Road to right, keep straight ahead. You are now angling northeast into the mountains over slowly rising rocky Class II and III road with a mesa nearby to the left and others further away to the right. Some old rock structures along the road. Vegetation sparse.

9.8 Small adobe ruin beside road.

10.1 First mountain palms appear on right, sparse.

11.1 Rock wall on right continues to parallel and cross road for several miles.

12.3 First irrigated fields appear on right as well as stream bed with trickle of water.

12.5 Enter narrow canyon, bend around into mountain valley while following narrow stream.

14.8 Old ruins.

15.7 More water, fields.

16.1 Easy crossing of stream.

17.4 Old San Miguel school and old dwelling on right.

17.6 Road left into San Miguel crosses date palm grove. .3 mile to village. Leaving San Miguel come back out same road and continue up valley to San José, past several buildings and farms. The gasoline pump is in San José.

20.0 Turnoff left to leave valley and the Comondus. Beyond here 4WD is required. But it is possible to go straight into San José from here, .2 straight ahead.

20.7 Pass by San José Cantina and begin climb out of valley. 1 mile up.

21.7 Reach plateau above green valley. Class IV with some Class V road.

34.0 Narrow road has reached a big flat. Low rolling hills and low cactus and brush are on all sides. The road has been generally good with some poor stretches and a rocky surface. The bends are sharp and some grades steep and slippery.

41.0 Class V and VI grade down; steep drop, sharp turns, big, loose rocks.

42.1 *Major Intersection*: You have just descended from the high plateau into a small valley. The road has passed a ranch on the left and straight ahead you drive right into a wall of a plateau and are faced with a T intersection. The sandy, hardpacked road to the right appears to be the main road, but is not; it goes 2 miles to the Rancho Viejo and reservoir, site of an old mission visiting station. The ranch is private and the road into it poor. At this intersection go left to reach the blacktop at Mex 1.

45.6 *Major Intersection*: Here five roads come together—an irritating problem for the weary driver. The correct road is hard to find, no matter where you are going. Best advice is to go straight and just ahead you will find yet another fork.

47.4 *Major Intersection*: A fork left to the La Purisima road, keep right.

48.6 *Major Intersection*: At this Y the road left goes to La Purisima and the road right goes to the blacktop. The road ahead is poor and the rocks large. This is the same stretch used going in to La Purisima from Ascencion. Expect Class IV with some V.

57.8 *Major Intersection*: Straight ahead to Rancho Rosarito at blacktop about 4 miles. Left to Rancho Canipole. Windmill and structure visible. Hard right for Ascencion and blacktop 3.7 miles.

61.5 Ascencion cafe and blacktop.

Expect Class I and II going in with some III.

Expect Class V and VI going out with some VII.

CANYON MISSION

San Javier: The third and southernmost of the mountain valleys containing hard to reach villages harbors one of Baja's well-preserved, majestic Jesuit missions. The second of the famous Baja missions, San Javier was built of stone in 1699 and remained active for 120 years.

A village surrounds the tall mission, and though there is no cafe, food and gasoline are available.

There is a caretaker at the mission, and its interior —domed ceiling, articulate woodworking, and simple altar—can be visited and photographed. A donation will help with protection and care of the mission.

Because the 22 miles of road to the mission are considered easy by the Mexicans, they offer taxi tours from Loreto. Although I've never seen a taxi in San Javier and doubt one could get in and out easily, I

San Javier, the second of Baja's missions, was founded in 1699 and the impressive structure which is still in use was started in 1744 and finished in 1758. According to some it is the most remarkable example of Baja mission architecture as it was conceived and executed under the direction of the Jesuit missionaries.

did follow an old 1942 Ford pickup into San Javier one dawn. Loaded down with workmen, it ground at one and two miles an hour through the tortuous canyon section (at 10 miles on the road-log) in a premier performance of grinning Mexican driving few Americans could have accomplished.

Once at the mission, loop out the easy way to Villa Insurgentes, 70 miles away over Class III road, or return to Loreto over the 22 miles of tough Class IV and V road.

This log will take the driver from the eastern entry to San Javier, and either out to the coast road down to Villa Insurgentes or up to the Comondus, which is a possible loop back to Mex 1 in four-wheel-drive. From Loreto to Loreto via San Javier and the Comondus, the distance is 201 miles. I once did it in one day on a Honda 360 roadbike in a dawn to dark endurance test. But I was lucky: Fewer cattle than usual were on the road that night.

Of course, the loop through La Purisima is also possible, but that one took me two days with an overnight in San Isidro. From Loreto to Loreto via San Javier and La Purisima, it is 223 miles.

No two of these mountain oases are alike; each town and village has a separate character, physical layout, and particular attraction. So if you can, visit all three of them. In San Javier the attraction is the mission, and the village of 200 people is clean and well kept.

LORETO TO SAN JAVIER MISSION TO THE WEST COAST HIGHWAY

MILE

0 **At the Pemex station just west of Loreto, one mile short of Mex 1, gas up and set your gauge at 0.**

6.0 **You have gone west from Loreto, turned left on Mex 1, and proceeded south a few hundred feet to the right turn, west, into the mountains marked by the sign: "San Javier." Drive in on Class II and III rocky, one-lane road with high mountains on all sides. Enter dry arroyo and work 6 miles into it.**

7.5 **After briefly leaving the arroyo the road returns to it.**

8.5 **Here some water begins to show in the riverbed. A cabin is on the left.**

9.0   **Enter narrow canyon; road to San Javier begins to wind and twist into these forbidding mountains.**

11.0   **Rancho alongside road.**

14.2   **Rancho, signs of old waterfalls.**

16.0   **Rancho.**

17.0   **Old road to right, to Comondus, is washed out, no longer in use. Do not attempt to use it.**

18.3   **Rancho.**

18.5   **Rancho.**

20.0   **Deep fork in river.**

21.5   **Enter San Javier. Mission at end of main street. Road winds right by mission and out of town to the left.**

24.8   **Rancho left, keep right.**

27.7   **Large shrine in canyon wall on left.**

28.1   **Rancho.**

34.1   **Rancho. From here, 30 miles of dusty Class II and III road out of mountains to dirt highway on ocean plain.**

65.9   **Dirt highway. Left for Villa Insurgentes and blacktop 18 miles. Right for Comondus, La Purisima, and other points north.**

Expect Class III to VI going in.
Expect Class II and IV going out.

A SHORT ADVENTURE

Santiago Loop: On the way to Cabo San Lucas is a stretch of old road that is not long enough to be a problem but is tough enough to provide a glimpse of the Baja that is disappearing. In a morning or afternoon one can travel easily to the four settlements along what used to be the main road.

On Mex 1 about 90 miles south of La Paz and 50 miles north of Cabo San Lucas, the turnoff, marked by a sign reading *Santiago*, runs west into the high mountains. The pavement continues two miles to the village, where Señor Cirilio Gomez runs a well-known grocery.

Cirilio, who once lived in Iowa, is a kind, patient man, and will give directions in English for the balance of the 15-mile loop back to Mex 1. Ask, too, about the other half of Santiago, for this village of 1000 people rests on two hills separated at a fair distance by an irrigated valley.

Gas, food, and lodging are available in Santiago, but nothing is fancy. Directed to a cafe on the plaza of the Loma Norte (North Hill), I entered the backyard of a dwelling, sat at the single, tilting table over an earth floor, and consumed the best chorizo and juevos Mexicanas in that part of Baja. A policeman joined me and in the rear, at the adobe oven, the hand preparation of corn tortillas continued as it has for centuries. In moments they were dropped hot before us onto the center of the old table. We smiled and ate with pleasure, alternating between thick chorizo and hot tortillas.

Out of Santiago beyond the Palamino Cantina, the road is Class II over the flats toward the crossroads village of Agua Caliente. To the right the high mountains of the Sierra de la Laguna or Victorias, purple in the distance, shimmer with the heat. To the left is low-lying sandy land between the Victorias and a chain of low mountains running beside the Pacific.

Not far from Santiago a large pump brings water from beneath the earth and sends it by ditch to the town. The large volume of water cascading into the dry desert is an unexpected sight, but the bone-thin cattle nearby gain precious little nourishment from it.

Agua Caliente is a small village of 100 persons set haphazardly among a grove of low trees. The road beyond deteriorates from Class II to some small stretches of Class III deep sand.

The road narrows and enters the former saddle-making and leather-working center of Miraflores, a long, narrow village of 800 people. A government attempt to revitalize the craft locally, after most of the artisans had fled to the opportunities of La Paz, has apparently failed, and the little blue stand, unattended and decaying out on Mex 1, is a depressing scene.

Food, gas, and lodging are available in Miraflores. Here you may exit to Mex 1, cutting the full loop short, or continue another two miles to Caduano. This small farming village has a number of interesting structures near the springs that irrigate the large grove of shade trees. From Caduano the dirt road swings two miles back to complete the loop at the pavement of Mex 1. In days past this was the only road to Cabo San Lucas.

SANTIAGO TO CADUANO VIA
MILE **MIRAFLORES AND AGUA CALIENTE**

0   **At turnoff west from Mex 1 to Santiago, set trip-gauge at 0.**

1.0   **Arrive Santiago at the main square and grocery. Gas on left coming in. Continue through and over hill to second part of town, then downhill into flats.**

2.0   **Water pump on right.**

6.5   **Agua Caliente. Go left in town center and work south out of village. Ahead you will encounter some relatively deep sand, Class III problem. Careful use of two-wheel-drive high-clearance vehicle should allow negotiation of this stretch.**

7.5   **Ranch lands to right, some fencing. Watch for cattle on road.**

11.4   **Road narrows and follows old riverbed into Miraflores. Road grade improves to Class II and takes left turn into village.**

11.8   **At grocery the town with its square and tiny plaza are to the left. Class II road to Caduano is to right. Left is to Mex 1 and pavement.**

14.8   **Caduano; springs, groves, well-kept old buildings.**

15.8   **Blacktop and Mex 1. Right to Cabo San Lucas, left to La Paz.**

Expect Class II with some III. Some deep sand between Agua Caliente and Miraflores.

MAGIC AT LAND'S END

Cabo San Lucas: It's a fair question: How can this part of Baja's expensive and well-known "Gold Coast" possibly be considered offbeat? The answer is easy. Most dirt-road travelers are intimidated by the name "Cabo San Lucas" and stories of the astounding extravagant hotels merged with the rocks of the cliffs. Unfortunately they pass the area by.

If you really want to do something "offbeat" after beating your way down the dreaded back roads of the desert peninsula, cough up $32 for one night in a double and treat yourself to Baja's outstanding architectural experience.

This place, where two seas meet; where like a mermaid the land narrows and slips smoothly into 300 feet of blue water; where Mexican dreamers have mingled tan rock with human habitation—and perhaps perfectly so with the two diverse but equally pleasing hotels—would be a terrific shame to miss.

The sandy beaches, the marlin and sailfish offshore, the sunsets and moonrises, the sleek ships at anchor in the tiny harbor—you will recognize the magic when you see it.

There is one trouble with Cabo San Lucas: At first glance it looks nothing like anyone's dream of a special place. After the 20-mile drive from San José Del Cabo, past impressive sweeping beaches, the line of famous rocks moving into the ocean is a dramatic sight. But the entry is dusty, the village tiny, and the government ferry dock and terminal desolate and barren.

MAGIC AT LAND'S END

Cabo San Lucas, where the Pacific meets the Sea of Cortez, and where Baja slips from sight into the sea, a small moon at sunset helps illuminate a tiny beach below high cliffs at Land's End.

The international gathering of yachts and luxury liners is hard put to overcome the first harsh impression of Cabo San Lucas. But a trip closer to the Finistierra Hotel, and then beyond it, over the low saddle separating the Sea of Cortez from the Pacific, to the equally startling and beautiful SolMar will excite appreciation, and all of Cabo San Lucas will be seen as the special place it is.

No Road Log for Cabo San Lucas. See pages 95 to 96 for areas near Cabo San Lucas on coast.

3

THE SEA OF CORTEZ SIDE

"For more than four centuries man has been trying to subdue the Baja Peninsula, physically or spiritually, to exploit it, or at least to make it do his bidding. For all this human effort most of the Peninsula clings stubbornly to its primitive state. Much of it remains as it was a thousand or perhaps even a million years ago."

William Weber Johnson,
Baja California, 1972

"A man 80 years old said to us: 'I've lived here all my life. You are the first visitors.' "

Erle Stanley Gardner,
Off the Beaten Track in Baja, 1967

"Being sent to hell by a Mexican cow is no idle possibility. My friend Manuel Empalme says 'In Mexico we call the cows God. They move for no man and sometimes they send him to hell if he drives too fast.' "

Jerry Kamstra,
Weed, 1974.

"Bad roads act as filters. They separate those who are sufficiently appreciative of what lies beyond the blacktop to be willing to undergo mild inconvenience from that much larger number of travelers which is not willing."

Eliot Porter in Joseph Wood Krutch's
The Forgotten Peninsula, 1961.

"One of the dividends of a trip by road down Baja California is the thrill of rising each morning with the knowledge that adventure is lurking somewhere ahead."

Erle Stanley Gardner,
Hovering over Baja, 1961.

THE GATEWAY

San Felipe: Reaching the eastern side of Baja is easy. Getting further south is not. If you come down from Mexicali there is pavement all the way to San Felipe. It's a route worth exploring. It runs straight south out of Mexicali and within 20 miles you are out of irrigated land and into hot, dry desert and bare gunmetal volcanic mountains that most people think represent all of Baja.

Not even a rare cactus grows on most of this land and in May the 120°-plus temperatures will fry your brains! Heat waves shimmer off the black pavement and off the hills and mirages are not uncommon. If you want to experience one of the harsher, more hostile portions of Baja—a real desert—this is it.

There is another way to reach San Felipe from the north: Leave Ensenada on Mex 16 which is paved to 10 miles east of Valle de Trinidad; from there it is 50 hot, dusty, mountain and desert miles to San Felipe on the east coast.

Once San Felipe was a simple fishing village, a few huts on the edge of a fine small crescent bay in the northern reaches of the Sea of Cortez. Giant, 300 pound Totuava were regularly hauled from the sea. Now San Felipe caters to tourists and hums and roars with motorcycles, dune buggies, and motorhome generators. And the Totuava are no more. Still, to get south you have to come here.

Once you're in the area, some of the dislikable aspects of San Felipe's Mardi Gras atmosphere can

The blacktop near Loreto typifies the excellent condition of Mex 1—the road which connects all the others in Baja.

be escaped, if you wish, by staking out a spot on one of the many beaches north and south of San Felipe. It costs $2 to $6 to lay your head down. There isn't a foot of beach around San Felipe that someone is not exploiting for money. Maybe that's not bad—it just means that not much around San Felipe is "offbeat."

There is no shortage of gas, food, and lodging in San Felipe, and the motels run the gamut, as a few minutes of driving will reveal. South of town there is nothing. Gasoline on this side of Baja has always been at a premium. If you want gas further south you had better buy *all you can carry* in San Felipe.

The dealer in Puertocitos is said to be having a problem getting his quota of gasoline. The rumor is true; he is often out. To be sure, there is some gasoline out there, but don't depend on finding it. And if you find it, don't bet on being able to buy it. I have in fact been able to buy gasoline at Alfonsina's fly-in resort on Gonzaga Bay, and across the bay at Papa Fernadez, her father's place. But the only gasoline you can really depend on after leaving San Felipe south is on the blacktop of Mex 1, 170 miles distant at Punta Prieta. Make sure you have enough to reach it.

If you have failed to buy anything in Mexicali, perhaps you will find it in San Felipe. However, there is nowhere in Baja to buy fishing equipment. You will find pieces here and there in San Felipe, but it is best to bring all you will need with you from the States.

At 14 miles south of Puertocitos the view is north back toward the rough passes. Rocky beaches line the deserted road.

THE ROUGH, TOUGH ROAD SOUTH

Puertocitos and Gonzaga Bay: Stories about this stretch of road are legion, and until that distant day when it will see rerouting and paving, the number of tales must continue to grow.

This back-breaker can either be in and out the same way or a loop trip down through Gonzaga Bay and out to the blacktop via Calamajue.

It is 51 miles in to Puertocitos, where there is a restaurant and grocery and there may be gas. A mod-est number of Americans live there but, except for its small clear bay, it is an unattractive place. The road to it is Class II and III. Very soon beyond Puertocitos the road rapidly goes bad in its 54 miles to Gonzaga. From Gonzaga it is 53 miles to the blacktop over Class III and IV winding desert roads.

There is a fine restaurant (by offbeat standards) at Alfonsina's on Gonzaga and one across the bay at Papa Fernadez. There are rooms at both places but no hot water. There are no groceries. These are lodges ready to serve fishermen and fly-in enthusiasts. Of course, the fishing is good. Camping is easy and free. Some fresh water is available at both resorts. It's a nice place.

South of Gonzaga Bay the road turns inland over the mountains to the blacktop near Punta Prieta. A good day's run is from Gonzaga out to Mex 1 and then, north of Punta Prieta, the turnoff back over to Bahia de Los Angeles.

Compared to what you have been over, the road out is good, Class III and IV with some spots of V. On the 50-mile stretch between Gonzaga and the blacktop there is nothing but a single small ranch, described in the following section.

Between San Felipe and Puertocitos, and between Puertocitos and Gonzaga particularly, there are

At dawn the sun rises over the Sea of Cortez at Alfonsina's resort and the thatched roofs are black against the morning sky. A small boat carries early morning fishermen.

enough undisturbed beaches and private bays and seemingly untouched places to last a busy man years. Forget your mechanical battle with the road long enough to visit them.

It's one hard day's driving to Gonzaga and another half-day out if you don't stop. It's possible to drive down to Puertocitos and back to San Felipe in one day.

Traffic on this road is light, though it is considered an alternate route south down Baja. That's pretty optimistic, and after you've seen the road you will know why. Many have come a long distance only to be turned back by the three terrible grades south of Puertocitos.

SAN FELIPE TO PUERTOCITOS & GONZAGA BAY

MILE

0 **Set trip-gauge at 0 at Pemex station in San Felipe. Road goes straight out of town on the sand flats above the sea. For some distance the sea is nearby and sometimes in sight to the left, but all access is through controlled beaches.**

102

THE SEA OF CORTEZ SIDE

4.8   Left turn to Estrella Beach.

14.5   Left turn to Percebu Beach (6.9 miles in): $3. This beach offers more to do than some others and is reached over a Class II sandy road. Some groceries for sale, several places to park campers and to pitch tents. Tides severe.

21.0   Santa Maria turnoff to left. Continue to wind inland from the ocean on a Class II and III rocky road over low rolling hills with some cactus and brush.

51.3   Puertocitos. Set your trip-gauge at 0 in the shade of the Pemex station and pray for good-luck. The road winds upward out of town to the right above the bay.

0   Leave Puertocitos south. Go immediately into hard bedrock surface, sharper bends, steeper grades, slippery gravel. Begin Class III and IV sections. 4WD not required but careful 2-wheel-driving needed. For a few miles out of town the road is bad, then improves.

11.2   Bad downgrade.

11.8   Bay to left.

13.6   Bad upgrade. This is the first of the terrible three. 2-wheel-drive pickups have made it through all three, and then turned around at Gonzaga and come back. 4WD would be better. A passenger car will not make it; a camper probably will not either. This is a Class IV grade, with some sections of V.

13.8   Top of first grade.

13.9   Bottom of first grade.

14.6   Beach to left, begin upgrade number 2, Class V with deep, rolling holes like waves in a river; the closer to the top, where the wheels do most of their spinning, the deeper the holes.

14.8   Top of second bad grade.

15.3   Bottom of second bad grade.

15.9   Begin upgrade number 3. Sections of this grade will severely jar the vehicle and can easily knock the axle off or break the oil pan. They are bedrock that has been eroded at the base; at one point, near the top of the grade, the bedrock simply ends: An eight inch wall of rock faces you in the middle of the road and there is nowhere to go but right over it. There is no stopping on these grades. If you lose momentum it means backing all the tortuous way back down. This is Class V grade with some Class VI. Remember, too, these grades are as treacherous going down as going up—if not more so.

16.9   Top of third grade, a long pull, and good view in all directions.

18.8   This is a bad grade going down: narrow; loose rock, deep holes, large buried rocks. Beach to left at bottom.

29.1   Beach to left. Begin climb up.

29.3   Top.

29.4   Beach to left. Bottom of grade.

30.0   Rancho to right.

32.0   First elephant trees.

33.5   Salvetierra to left, closed.

46.1   Left turn to Papa Fernandez on Gonzaga Bay. 2 miles.

52.2   Alfonsina's, after making left turn off road at 50 mile. Marked by sign.

Expect Class II to IV generally but very difficult grades out of Puertocitos; Classes V and VI there.

CALAMAJUE

Calamajue River and Ruins via Las Arrastras: After you have fished and explored both sides of Gonzaga Bay and taken the short drives to Punta

CALAMAJUE

Francisco and Guadalupe, children of Manuel Cantrera see few tourists.

Final, Molino De Lacy, and the end of the road there, it is time to leave the Sea of Cortez and work over the mountains back to Mex 1.

There are four attractions along this 50-mile stretch of Baja back-country road. First are the boulders encountered after leaving the Gonzaga Bay and heading inland. Following that, the tiny ranch and turquoise mine at Las Arrastras, at an unassuming, tumbledown turn in the road, is a place to stop to meet Manuel Cantrera and his family.

For a time Manuel worked as a laborer in Tijuana, but he did not like the effect the large city was having on his children. Now, working the little mine south and west of the ranch, he brings out blue crisicola and green turquoise that he displays on paper plates in a little entryway in his home. He patiently works all the gems by hand; they are for sale at a dollar each.

Down in the gully behind the home is a tall tower and beneath it a deep well of cold, clear water. At the edge of the rocks is a crank and windlass to lower a five-gallon bucket into the cool depths.

"Do you want a shower?" Manuel asked me in Spanish as I was looking at his display of turquoise and crisicola. It had been a dusty ride from Gonzaga and I had slept the previous two nights on the beach next to the motorcycle. It was a very hot day in May.

I looked around and assumed he was making a joke. But I said, "Un lluvia? Si, con mucho gusto."

Manuel's son Francisco jumped up and led me down the dirt trail to the tower. One hundred feet behind me and up the hill I saw the younger children giggling. This is it, I thought. As my old grandfather said, "If they haven't seen it before it's something new, and if they have it's something old." And with his advice in mind I stripped down and stood under the tower, my untanned parts glistening white in the bright hot sun. Francisco cranked the windlass and up came five beautiful wet gallons of wellwater. Standing with legs slightly spread for stability I took the 40 pounds of bucket and water and held it over my head, cascading it full and refreshing over my face, shoulders, and body. What a feeling! Desert all around, and water pouring full over your head.

Francisco and I continued with a 25 gallon shower. Within minutes after the last bucket the sun had dried me. I dressed and went refreshed up the hill. The whole world felt an enormously better place.

"Cuanto es para la lluvia?" I asked Francisco.

"Nada, gratis," Francisco said.

"For free! Fantastic!" I told him.

"You have sweets?" Francisco asked me in Spanish.

I had none, but Francisco and his sister and brother helped with some photography and were paid.

Las Arrastaras, where a shower is more valuable than jewelry, is a place to stop. If not for one then for the other.

The third attraction along this lonely, twisting Class III road is the river water, alkaline as it is, that comes in surprising volume down Arroyo Calamajue. There are multiple crossings, none difficult, allowing the off-roader to splash water and the biker to get thoroughly and delightfully soaked in the desert heat. So that day it was two showers, one clothed and one not.

Just as you enter this arroyo of moving water you come also upon the site of the old mission. A road leads to it across the river and slightly downstream on the east side. The site of an old mine is on the west side. The riverbed here runs northeast.

All that is left of the mission is the site. It is marked by a small sign and an outline of native rock.

If you come in from Mex 1 these 50 miles can be completed in less than three hours and that's the same for coming back out of Gonzaga. It's a trip well worth making. The only services are at Gonzaga.

GONZAGA TO LAS ARRASTARAS
MILE   TO CALAMAJUE TO MEX 1

0 Set trip gauge at 0 at Alfonsina's restaurant and airstrip.

6.5 Traveling south, after a left turn out of Alfonsina's, you come at this mileage to a 4-way intersection. Left to Punta Final and Molino De Lacey, a 10-mile loop back to this point on Class II and III road. Straight ahead to dead-end 4 miles. Right turn to leave Gonzaga and cross mountains to Mex 1. This log makes right turn.

9.5 You are moving west on a sandy, rutted Class III road winding slowly into higher mountains. There is a road right but keep left. The sea is behind you. Some cactus begin.

14.0 First stand of elephant trees.

16.0 First stand of big cardon cactus. Dramatic geographic change from level, alluvial fan of the east coast to jumbled, boulder-filled ridges.

22.1 Rancho Las Arrastaras, Manuel Cantrera, turquoise, well. No services. Coffee may be offered during business.

22.5 Rough road right to Mex 1 via Rancho Chapala and Laguna Chapala. Class V and VI, thick dust, 17.3 miles to Mex 1, not recommended except for road-baggers. Keep straight.

28.5 Road left to Ejido Galiano and small beach on Sea of Cortez reached by Class IV and V road down the dry bed of the Calamajue River. It is 17.2 miles in and the same back out. No services. Keep straight.

34.2 Lone tree on left side of barren stretch of straight road offers shade and place to rest.

39.2 Enter canyon and note green grass, mission site to left, mine to right. Water running down center of road. Road follows riverbed. You will cross and recross the wide, shallow pools of this river many times. The water lasts for about 8 miles until the road leaves the canyon and improves upstream. Watch for cattle. In the mountains near the water, mountain sheep persist, but without a guide are rarely seen.

44.2 Canyon diminishes, water disappears.

45.7 Branch right to Mex 1. Six miles by this longer route to Mex 1; the road goes north for some distance before making a sharp left to Mex 1. It is better to continue on straight here to the junction with Mex 1 adjacent to Rancho El Crucero. This is Class II road with some parts III. The right turn is Class III with some IV.

53.0 Rancho El Crucero corral and ranch buildings to the right below a curve of Mex 1 with white railing. This is the blacktop. There are no services at this rancho but once on a Sunday I repaired a flat there and no cowboy was complete without assisting. Gas is 10 miles to the left at Punta Prieta parador and the Bahia de Los Angeles turnoff. It is 60 miles north to the El Presidente Motel at Cataviña. It is 50 miles south and east to Bahia de Los Angeles.

Expect Class III with some small sections of IV and V.

BAHIA DE LOS ANGELES

Bahia de Los Angeles: Once reached only by dirt road, this large island-filled bay is rich with possibilities. It is 40 paved miles off Mex 1 and once there

BAHIA DE LOS ANGELES

the motel, store, and cantina complex operated by Antero Diaz make you glad you came. There is a Pemex station, a large runway, and roads north and south to explore. There is charter service from San Diego and Los Angeles and boats and fishing tackle are for rent.

Yet Bahia de Los Angeles is a small place and retains its relaxed, unhurried character. Dinners are family style and once a week there's turtle steak. Since Erle Stanley Gardner often headquartered here in his explorations between the 1940s and 1970s, you will find his pictures and remarks well displayed.

With wild sheep in the mountains and fish in the waters, the aura of sportsmen and of outdoor accomplishments dominates. But it is not a negative domination, and any traveler will feel welcome and relaxed in the presence of Antero Diaz's easy, confident hospitality.

A motel room on the beach with hot water is $15. Supper is $6, breakfast $3.

High blue-gray peaks rear up behind Bahia de Los Angeles, and if you don't wish to camp near the relatively noisy center of activity there are deserted beaches both north and south that Antero can direct you to. Sometimes there will be a small fee, sometimes not.

The high mountains hold lion as well as sheep, and on the lower flats coyote are common. The big bay is protected from the power of the Sea of Cortez by the giant island of De La Guarda, 40 miles long with peaks over 4000 feet high. Closer to shore other islands offer fishing anchorages and places to explore. All are barren.

This area, along with several others south down the length of the Sea of Cortez, has become a favorite of kayaking enthusiasts. Afternoon winds present a problem, but the mornings offer calm water. One intrepid paddler had reached Loreto in his small kayak when I met him in 1975. He had been gone 30 days from San Felipe and told tales of beaches and lagoons and diving that held each of us at the small cafe table spellbound. His goal was La Paz, and undoubtedly, some 60 days later, he reached it.

This cholla is growing on a boulder near Bahia Los Angeles.

The beginning of the road south, described on page 78, goes to the ruins of the Las Flores Mine 10 miles out. This silver mine was closed down in 1912, during the most recent Mexican Revolution. But between that time and 1889, when the mine was opened by American interests, it produced over $2,000,000 in silver ore. There once was a 2½-mile-long wire tramway into the mountains and seven miles of narrow-gauge railroad.

At the north end of the bay the road comes to an end after a few miles. But don't let that stop you from going up there. You will find some unspoiled beaches and clear diving and fishing water you will be a long time forgetting.

There are trailer parks and to the north areas, as yet unspoiled, that will take motorhomes and trailers. Parking is free. In Bahia de Los Angeles the parks closeby the runway are $5 a night and offer showers and partial hookups.

MILE   BAHIA DE LOS ANGELES: LOCAL

0   Set trip-gauge at 0 at Casa Diaz or Pemex station. South 9.9 according to "Three Old Mining Towns" section (p. 76). If you go only to the mine site and begin to return, you will have 9.9 on your gauge there. Turning around and heading back you will come to:

14.4   Turn right at this point to visit the picturesque deserted south end of Los Angeles Bay. Drive on hardpacked mud flats, avoiding sandy cutoffs. Reach a long, wide aircraft runway used as an alternate when the downdrafts at Casa Diaz get unmanageable.

18.1   Reach curving lagoon, new unoccupied building offers shade. In front is a fine long, sandy beach with small waves. Road continues on 2 miles to its end where there is additional, very private camping for a low daily fee to Antero Diaz.

0   Set trip-gauge at 0 at Casa Diaz or Pemex station. Go north the way you came in over pavement and toward the trailer parking area. When the pavement takes a sharp right down to the bay and the parking area, keep straight, north, on the Class II road into the brush and sandy desert. This narrow dirt road parallels the bay for several miles north.

2.0   Road splits often with entries to beach. The 15 camp spots along this stretch can be reached by motorhomes, campers, and autos. There is no charge but some of the beach is rocky rather than sandy.

7.5   Mild deterioration of road; Class III. Road begins to work to right.

9.0   Reach Punta La Gringa and the green sheds of a fishing cooperative. Pass by with care. Private property. Arrive at beach with several camping areas on each side of a long spit. Very clear blue-green water. Wind may sometimes blow hard. Over the hill to the left are more beaches. A 4WD trail winds over. Clamming and fishing are both good.

Expect Class II and III.

North of La Gringa: Beyond the spit at La Gringa are several meandering motorcycle and four-wheel-drive tracks, all leaving and returning at the same point: the green buildings of the fishing cooperative.

The area north of La Gringa is fun to explore. There is no danger of getting lost, and the many roads and side roads lead to several fine beaches that never seem to have any campers, perhaps because this area is 10 miles from the store and center of activity at Bahia Los Angeles.

The fishing is good; the pelican watching and photographic opportunities with island and bay and mountain backdrops excellent; and for the nighttime buff the La Gringa area assures, when the small fish school up and jump, some real pelican action. A flashlight will trigger events if the moon or stars do not.

Daylight exploration along the beaches will reveal shells and starfish and various species of coral. Robert Western found three brightly colored coral specimens in just a few minutes. One was chalky white, the other a light magenta, and the third a bright golden yellow.

The longest road goes to an abandoned copper mine and ends at a striking arroyo that winds an additional three miles to a deserted beach on the Sea of Cortez, a beach unfortunately rocky if rewarding in drift. Probably this beach is never visited. The hour walk to it down this twisting arroyo deep within canyon walls is both eerie and interesting, with striking rock formations, in particular one granite outcropping at the end, down which the hiker must twist over rock in the shape of an amusement park slide.

North from Punta La Grina; the sharp outline of Isla Coronado in the foreground and the 40 mile long Isla La Guarda in the background.

BAHIA DE LOS ANGELES

From time to time it is necessary to climb around what must be high waterfalls when it rains.

The arroyo empties, with a sharp curve, onto a wide, flat alluvial fan of sand and cactus. Its firm base allows easy walking to the beach a half-mile distant. For the pleasure of knowing at least one part of Baja intimately and with the certain knowledge that few do, this walk and the tranquillity it brings are recommended.

MILE	NORTH OF LA GRINGA
0	At the green buildings of the fishing cooperative on La Gringa spit.

Several roads wind from here over the hills to the north. No log could catalog them all. They are all short and lead to beaches and hilltops all in the same vicinity.

The road to the mine goes northwest from the fishing camp up a wide arroyo directly away from the bay and past several piles of fishing cooperative garbage and sea shells. |
1.9	Fork right, keep straight. Fork goes back over to La Gringa beaches.
3.3	Class IV grade up .5.
3.5	Narrow grade.
4.1	Enter tiny enclosed valley from which there seems no exit.
4.4	Cross dry bed of white arroyo.
5.5	Leave valley over steep grade. This is a 30 percent Class VII up for .5 of a mile. Just beyond the top of this grade you wind along the side of a cliff on a narrow cut; ahead you see the mine and mine cuts in the side of a large hill. The road will drop into an arroyo at the foot of the mine, one fork goes right up to the mine area and dead-ends on the hill; the other goes down in the arroyo, where it dead-ends—although a branch of it goes up on a little shelf above the arroyo

to the left and dead-ends there. An old frame building once occupied the shelf.

| 7.7 | Road ends in arroyo below mine. Some tracks continue down arroyo where the curious have attempted to keep going to the bitter end. Don't bother. It is impossible. Some trail bike tracks make it about a mile and they have to give up at the first big waterfall. |

The walk to the sea can be made in 2½ hours round-trip with some time for beachcombing and resting.

Expect Class II to IV going in with some short stretches of VI and VII.

San Borja Mission, the unexpected gift: It looks easy on a map and some travelers will tell you it is, but the ride to this well-preserved mission is over rough road. Nevertheless, it is worth every minute of the effort.

The 200-year-old stone church is one of Baja's high-ranking ruins, and the adobe walls adjacent to it date back to 1759, when the mission was first being laid out.

San Borja is striking and surprising because although it is a ruin it is almost entirely intact. And after seeing the beauty of missions like San Ignacio, Loreto, and San Javier it is easy to imagine what San Borja must have looked like when it was abandoned early in the nineteenth century.

Although San Borja is usually a side trip from Bahia de Los Angeles and can be seen by going in and out the same day, the ruins really deserve a less hurried inspection. Since it is easy to camp next to or in the church, and since such camping would disturb none of the five people who live in the nearby adobe homes, an overnight stay at this beautiful mission is an enjoyable experience.

The lattice work over San Borja's doors have become a familiar Baja landmark.

The walls, the spiral staircase, the high ceiling, the interior stonework and the interior and exterior detail all take hours of study; and to see them in different lights is rewarding.

There are two ways to reach the church, and each is 22 miles in and 22 back out, but not necessarily over the same road. The entrance from Bahia de Los Angeles, definitely the rougher of the two, goes over some rocky stretches of road, and in and out of some rough arroyos.

There are no facilities of any kind at the old mission site. It is completely deserted, though local residents do use it as a place of worship. Gas is available at Rosarito and Bahia de Los Angeles, so no matter where you start the 44-mile journey there is gas at the other end.

But if you plan to reach Bahia de Los Angeles via San Borja when you are moving north up the peninsula don't do it as a shortcut. It is far easier to stay on the blacktop all the way to Bahia de Los Angeles. On a map the road to San Borja may seem shorter in miles—and it is—but it is a great deal longer in hours and is much more wear and tear on the vehicle. Take this shortcut only if you planned on seeing the mission anyway. And allow six hours of driving time from Rosarito to Bahia de Los Angeles. The same applies, of course, if you are going south. Those 44 miles will take you six hours.

BAHIA DE LOS ANGELES
MILE   TO ROSARITO VIA SAN BORJA

0   **At 44 kilometer sign north of Bahia de Los Angeles on the Mex 1 cutoff blacktop. For entry from Rosarito to Bahia de Los Angeles reverse this log.**

2.1   **Road to left, keep right. Road left ends in canyon.**

5.7   **Road right to rancho, keep straight ahead.**

10.8   **Summit. Impressive stands of cardon cactus and cirio trees.**

14.8   **Dim track to right, to Rancho San Ignacito, bypasses the mission. Not recommended for any purpose.**

15.4   **Class IV upgrade .2.**

15.6   **Rancho road left, keep right.**

20.8   **Reach valley with mission. Road goes directly to mission and turns into parking area adjacent. At mission road forks to right to continue to Rosarito.**

26.8   **Rancho on right.**

29.5   **Road goes left, keep right.**

40.2   **Rancho on left.**

41.9   **Large round corral on left.**

42.5   **Rosarito and blacktop of Mex 1. Gas, food, groceries available.**

        Expect Class II to IV to San Borja.
        Expect Class II to III from San Borja to Rosarito.

SAN FRANCISQUITO

San Francisquito and El Barril: Reaction to San Francisquito, the resort, and El Barril, the rancho to the south, varies. As the brochure says of the fledgling resort: "No telephones, no highways, no television, just miles of sandy beach, your cabaña and you." And that's the truth!

These places are reached either by driving south and east from Guerrero Negro to El Arco, where the road in begins, or by coming south over the far more difficult and dangerous route from Bahia de Los Angeles.

It is 50 miles in and 50 out. A person could go in and out in one day, but it wouldn't make sense to do so. The route from Bahia de Los Angeles is slightly longer and would take at least all day just to reach one or the other. Each destination is 12 miles from a fork

Signs are rare in Baja so when you see one you find it impressive. This effort is just out of Pozo Aleman on the way to the isolated beach of San Francisquito on the Sea of Cortez.

In March and April the fishing for yellow-tail is good around San Francisquito, where gear and boats can be rented.

The road's reputation for difficulty is kept alive by the real terrors of the Cuesta de la Ley, "The Grade That Rules." Before and after that real hurdle the run to San Francisquito and El Barril is not hard, but this .5 of a mile between El Arco and the sea is why you will need a good four-wheel-drive vehicle for both directions.

For all but the last 12 miles to San Francisquito, you will be guided by the signs to El Barril, the first of which appears in Pozo Aleman, 2.3 miles out of El Arco. If you turn right for El Barril and make the run down to the ranch first, you meet the Villavicencio brothers whose pictures appear often in Erle Stanley Gardner's books. Both stand well over six feet tall, and one is six feet seven.

They run a tight ranch and do well with cattle. Their plans to make a resort out of the ranch have never materialized; there are no services at all. You can get water, and if you need to camp for a night on the beach in the palm grove it can be arranged.

If you want the kind of isolation that gives the stars at night a pulse of life you hadn't thought they could possess, and gives you sense of being a thousand miles from anywhere and everywhere, then San Francisquito is your place.

If there are no other guests, and very often there are not, there will be Pepe behind the tiny bar in that cabaña and Lupe in the kitchen-cabaña—and you. And at night: the blackness, the sea, and the stars.

in the road, one straight ahead to the coast and the other slightly south.

After grinding in the 50 miles from El Arco, if the left fork is taken, for San Francisquito, the traveler will find a gathering of seven cabañas around a thatched-roof bar and kitchen set on cement foundations, and will ask himself, "Is this it?"

San Francisquito, as its name implies, is tiny. The population is two: Pepe the all-around man and Lupe the all-around woman. Beyond San Francisquito, over the saddle of sand, which when I was there in 1976 was swallowing an abandoned four-wheel-drive, is a tiny, almost landlocked bay and a fishing village of 20 persons who want nothing to do with any tourists.

Back at the resort the meals are good but by Baja standards expensive: breakfast $4, lunch $5, and dinner $7.50. Gasoline, if there is enough left after planes have refueled, is $1 per gallon. A cot and sleeping bag in an unwalled cabaña cost $8 for a single and $10 for a double. Pepe can point you up or down the beach to a spot that might cost you less or perhaps even nothing.

SAN FRANCISQUITO AND
EL BARRIL VIA EL ARCO

MILE

0 **Having come 26 miles from Mex 1 into El Arco and proceeded about 200 feet beyond the yellow grocery on the left, set trip-gauge at 0 as dirt road leaves blacktop. Drop off pavement to left down steep arroyo. Wind out of town through maze of dwellings, fol-**

lowing your best guess as to the "main" road. Work through narrow rocky, one-lane road.

2.3 Pozo Aleman. Now you know you selected the right roads. Old mining town, good to stop and explore. Sign on far horizon, placed by Rancho El Barril. Second green sign, placed by San Francisquito, indicates same road for both. Go straight out of Pozo Aleman and wind into hills.

10.0 You have been winding in the low hills. A ranch road will go to the left, keep straight.

14.7 Cross steep arroyo, down and then up, poor; reach boojum tree area.

19.7 Cross steep arroyo, down and then up: poor, Class V.

20.1 Short, difficult upgrade, Class IV.

20.3 Rock corral of expert design and workmanship on left.

23.1 Ranch to left. Another rock corral. Set against a lonely rocky hill, a deserted building, its door flapping and its sheet metal creaking in the wind, suggests what it must have been like to struggle to survive here and to fail. To imagine this is to begin to understand the character not only of the Californianos but of Mexicans. This might be the loneliest spot in Baja California.

28.0 Road drops off plateau and begins to deteriorate to Class IV.

29.0 Mild beginning of La Cuesta de la Ley. The next mile is what this road is all about.

29.2 You have climbed up over rocks imbedded deeply in earth, sharp gray-black granite covered with loose white sand, and between narrow, enclosing sides of the road and sharp cactus growing close by. Your tires spin and the grade is steep. A closed gate blocks your way. The sea is before you, a steep canyon to your left. Rocks rise sharp-

ly to your right. Secure your vehicle and open the gate; after passing through carefully lock it again. The lock is manual.

Now you will go down the worst part of the grade. Large rocks, broad deep holes, sharp turns, dangerous dropoffs, and slippery sand. Even the steady shovel-maintenance of El Barril cowboys can't keep up with this. But it sure helps.

29.7 Bottom of La Cuesta. You have squirmed down .5 mile of rough grade over which you will have to travel to exit. Some believe it is worth it to attempt the bad road north to Bahia de Los Angeles just to miss La Cuesta de la Ley. Don't believe it. La Cuesta is bad but it is quickly over with. The same is not true of the alternate route out.

35.2 Right turn to El Barril. Keep straight here for San Francisquito even though main road seems to go to right. Go right for El Barril 12 miles over similar road. Class III to coast. This log goes to San Francisquito.

36.0 Here is the left turn for the alternate route out, the rough road north to Bahia de Los Angeles suitable only for 4WD and dune buggies.

36.7 Road from El Barril joins with road to San Francisquito.

48.7 You have driven 12 miles over rocky cactus-covered, rolling hills near the unseen sea. The timber entry arch is flanked by barbed wire. Cabañas are in view to the right, on the edge of the beach. Most of the maze of roads to the right go to the beach and the tiny resort. The road straight ahead goes to the airport, then up and over a low saddle to the fishing camp 2 miles ahead.

Expect Class II and III with some IV, with VII and VIII on La Cuesta de la Ley only.

ROUGH AND READY CITY

Santa Rosalia: Avoided by tourists because of its reputation as a working mill town; its rough edges no one is ready to remove; and its old buildings unchanged since the late nineteenth century, when French interests controlled the mine and influenced the town's architecture and manners; Santa Rosalia is without a doubt one of Baja's special places.

From the moment the road into town winds through the edge of the great copper mill, within a hundred feet of the fiery interior furnaces, to the later hour when you find solace on the plaza between the large Palacio Municipal and the wooden Benito Juarez Secondary School—all of it beneath large green trees and overhanging wooden balconies—you will know why the town sticks in the memory of so many travelers.

It was to Santa Rosalia once the center of a copper boom, that kidnaped Yaqui Indians from the Mexican State of Sonora were shipped to work and die in mine gangs. Today the production of copper continues.

There are only 10,000 people here, but the town seems larger. And Santa Rosalia is not a plastic town; it is not out to impress or catch any tourist. From its hundreds of wooden balconies, to its board sidewalks, its unusual metal church (an accident of international shipping left it here rather than in France after its display at the 1890 World's Fair), stone walls, dirty black bay, blistering heat, and steep barren hills, Santa Rosalia is itself.

The harbor is dirty; as far back as 1935 in his book *Flight of the Least Petrel*, Griffing Bancroft was saying, "dirtiest place I ever saw."

So many pass Santa Rosalia by because of its reputation as a rough city and because the pleasures of Concepcion Bay and the tourist town of Mulege wait so closely to the south.

In this town of two long, narrow main streets, all services are available. But none are tourist oriented, so here at last a person can begin to feel that he is in Mexico.

It is an active town and its hum and rhythm are unmistakable. Banks, stores, groceries, business

The old Central Hotel is a Santa Rosalia landmark while in the background smoke from the copper mill fills the sky.

offices, and a theater occupy the old wooden buildings. The Post Office might have been in Kansas in 1870.

On Third Street the small bookstore run by Ruben Nuñez Brooks is a good place to get instructions. Ruben, who buys often in the States, speaks English. He also carries a small supply of camera film.

But this unselfconsciousness is probably doomed. The first modern motels are being built just south of town and undoubtedly the future holds more. What will become of Santa Rosalia's structures, some of which are still active, is anyone's guess.

For side trips from Santa Rosalia see page 79.

THE OTHER SIDE OF CONCEPCION BAY

Concepcion is the best-known of Baja's beautiful places. Its white sands and clear blue-green waters attract many tourists who come for the superb fishing, excellent diving, or relaxed camping. And when Concepcion becomes crowded, as its six separate bays often do, there are always those restless few whose eyes wander across the wide stretch of enclosed waters silently wondering, What is over there on the other side?

At the end of the road on the other side of Concepcion Bay some fine hidden beaches, old mine ruins, and coastline rarely explored from land await the adventurous traveler.

No map indicates any road. No book describes what is or might be over there.

Many will be surprised to learn that along the other side of Concepcion there is a road, and that it travels the full 30 miles of bayshore to the furthest point. It is an adventurous road, a challenge to negotiate and explore, and it leads to many beaches and unknown parts of the Concepcion Peninsula.

The run along the bay's east side parallels the shore as it works north below the high peaks of the Concepcion mountains. At the end, just before the point, there is a 10-mile side road up an arroyo and over the mountains and down a second arroyo to the Sea of Cortez side.

This relatively easy "Baja 30 miles" in and out can be accomplished in a single day by starting early and returning in the dark. But for this exploration it's better to plan on camping overnight.

However, and sadly so, the lower, gentler heights of the eastern shore are no match for the dramatic mountain-backed bays and beaches of El Coyote, El Requeson, and the other famous Concepcion beaches on the western shore.

So if you are already packing to hurry across on this unknown road to find another Concepcion, you will be disappointed: There is only one Concepcion in Baja and it is already in use. But if your idea is to go over and travel a virtually untraveled road, to explore beaches and tidal pools that no one visits, to plot on the point some four-wheel-drive pathways of your own, to find sea shells in great quantities and canyons and arroyos getting little or no use, then don't hesitate.

The shore fishing is relatively good, but does not compare with that of the known parts of Concepcion. Camping is on an open plain until the point, and there is wood all along the way. And as on the west side the eastern shore does get wind.

At the end of the road there is an unusual find. After a winding trip on the 10-mile-cutoff over the mountains of the Concepcion Peninsula and down an arroyo to the Sea of Cortez, a tiny cove, sandy beach, and rock-lined well are reached. In the distance both north and south are evidence of other coves and beaches. But the unexpected waits around the rocky point to the north.

Meandering unsuspectingly out to that point to check what is beyond, the wanderer shakes his head in disbelief. For in the distance, where nothing but rocky coast should be, are thousands of square feet of old mining foundations and the ruins of a once large mine—a government attempt many years past to extract valuable magnesium from the mineral-rich area. The ruins are not on any map and so they come as a complete surprise.

Like the first, this second, hidden cove with the mine ruins, contains a fine sandy beach. On the shore of the Sea of Cortez, the entire mine site is now a mass of cement and wood rubble. There are many foundations intact and several winding roads, but no structures remain whole. To explore well both the coves and ruins and the additional beaches north and south would mean camping at least one night here, and the spot makes a good breaking point in a two-day journey.

Expect Class II and III roads going in with some Class IV going over the hill to the hidden coves and mine site. There are very few sections of Class V on this route, but four-wheel-drive or a motorcycle would certainly simplify the run.

THE OTHER SIDE OF CONCEPCION BAY

MILE

0 At the southern end of Concepcion Bay, at the sign indicating Rancho Santa Rosalita and a water project, set trip-gauge at 0. There are cement block buildings near the turn-in. Another turn-in just north of this point dead-ends at a fishing camp on the southern shore of Concepcion Bay.

3.4 Having passed the block structures you are heading east along the southern shore of Concepcion and now pass through groves of tall cardon cactus. There is a fork to the right to Rancho Sebastian and just ahead another fork to the right. Keep straight ahead at each fork and when in doubt try to parallel beach. Turkey vulture and pelican activity is common in this area.

4.3 Fishing camp on first portion of east shore of Concepcion. Drive beyond it along water's edge of rocky beach. The long run north begins here.

6.0 Fishing camp in shelter of small trees. Road goes straight through, continuing north.

12.0 Road leaves beaches and moves inland. Doves prominent all along road. For several miles road swings to and away from beach but is never a great distance from the water.

14.0 Fishing camp on beach; road right to Rancho San Ignacito, keep straight.

14.8 Larger fishing camp with some structures on beach in grove of trees, go straight by.

15.0   Fork right is one entry to Rancho El Salto, keep straight.

15.8   Road winds inland to Rancho El Salto, located above to the right on a low plateau. The large peak Cerro Colorado is behind the ranch to the east. Just before the ranch, and while still down in the tree-filled, sandy, rocky arroyo, a very dim track switches back to the left. This is the continuing road north; if you cannot locate it, someone at the ranch will show it to you.

19.3   Having followed the dim track that shows more cattle tracks than tire tracks, you will enter and pass through several wide dry salt flats just up from the beach.

22.7   Road parallels beach.

23.2   Road parallels beach. Good spot to pick up driftwood for later fire. However, if camp is to be at end of road, there is plenty of wood there.

23.5   Several crescent beaches.

25.7   Crescent beach.

26.7   Road moves out onto beach and beach rocks. Careful with tides.

27.7   Small clear bay.

28.0   Road leaves beach. Long straight stretch inland.

29.1   Road returns to beach and small bay.

29.6   Road leaves beach.

29.7   *Major Intersection*: T intersection as road drops into arroyo. Road left continues a few hundred feet in arroyo, then climbs out, continues to the point. In the area of the point the road left disappears and begins to meander in several different tracks. There are about two more miles of road ahead to several beaches if you go left. If you go right in this arroyo:

30.7   Road goes up narrow but sandy firm-based arroyo, twisting left and right into the mountains.

31.7   Arroyo begins to narrow with high walls on left side.

32.5   Climb out of arroyo and wind over low rise to opposite drainage.

33.5   Rock well to right, bucket and rope, cove straight ahead.

34.0   End of road. Old road to mine site climbs over saddle to left. Some ruins here of old rancho.

Expect Class II and III on this entire run with some short stretches and climbs of IV and V.

SAN BRUNO: THE OLD COLONY SITE

Just 14 years before the historic landing, in 1697, of the Jesuit missionaries at Loreto, an earlier significant attempt had been made to colonize the peninsula just a few miles north of Loreto. This earlier colonizing effort, made before the hostile land was awarded by a dismayed crown to the Jesuits, was to be a failure, even though the undertaking involved not only civilians but soldiers and administrators as well, and was led by Admiral Isidro de Atondo y Antillion. According to the Baja historian Pablo L. Martinez of La Paz, Atondo "was endowed with all that was indispensable by the royal exchequer, with two ships as well as provisions and troops."

Atondo had given up an effort to establish the colony at La Paz when the Indians rebelled against his treatment of them. Martinez writes that Atondo then "ran about for some time, looking over islands, and finally after having been on the other coast [the Mexican mainland] for provisions, he steered toward the site that he desired, disembarking his men at the place now known as San Bruno on the 6th of October [1683]."

SAN BRUNO: THE OLD COLONY SITE

The beach at San Bruno is along the alternate route south of Santa Rosalia on the way to Mulege.

In the small valley they chose, they "founded the Real in triangular form, with a stone cannon at each corner. Inside they constructed a church, a house for troops, and a warehouse." During the nearly two years it flourished, the little colony was the base for many important explorations, including one by the expedition cosmographer, who was later to become a famous Mexican missionary, the Austrian Jesuit Padre E. F. Kino. He reached the Pacific and discovered the spring and river and green valleys of La Purisima.

An unusually dry year coupled with insufficient provisions and poor health all led to the colony's failure, and on May 8, 1685 Atondo was ordered to abandon the effort. No further attempts were made to colonize the peninsula, and the dry land began its 12-year wait for the energetic Jesuits who would become the first to gain a firm foothold on its shores and interior mountains.

It is difficult today to locate the exact site of the San Bruno Colony, but its proximity to the blacktop of Mex 1 makes the exciting search possible.

There are two equally suitable entrances to Rancho Buena Vista, the rancho closest to the site; one entry is 20 kilometers north of Loreto and the other 25. The rancho is two miles from the beach at the Sea of

SAN BRUNO: THE OLD COLONY SITE

Cortez near Punta Mangles. At the beach beyond the rancho are a small fishing camp and a large lagoon directly behind a rocky overlook. Atondo landed north of this spot, and to reach the arroyo leading to the San Bruno site one begins at Rancho Buena Vista.

A dim track leads from the rancho yard northeast through the brush two miles to a small, high-post corral on the edge of a wide, deep arroyo, which at this point runs east and west. The corral is on the south side.

Travel by vehicle is not possible beyond this point, but motorcycles could proceed easily through the corral and down the earth ramp to the arroyo. The ramp is a blind into which cattle are hearded into the corral. The entry is too narrow for even a small auto to slip through.

There is no trail in the arroyo, but about one mile west up the arroyo is a series of small hills overlooking both the arroyo and its surrounding valleys. This is the probable area of the San Bruno site, on the north side of the arroyo.

Photographer Western and I spent a day on foot climbing the hills and searching the valleys for any sign of the old colony. An old trail was found, as well as some piles of stones suggesting work by human hand, but more searching must be done here before an exact location is reported.

The ranchers claim to know the ruins and insist all that is there is the pile of rocks. We think more can be found. Because of heavier than average rainfall the year of our visit, there was a large significant water hole in the arroyo directly below the pile of stones, which was no more than a 100 feet above and back from the arroyo.

The turnoff for Rancho Buena Vista, 15 miles north of Loreto and 70 south of Mulege, is negotiated easily in a pickup. It is Class II and III all the way except for the very first part of the north entry, where

This post corral is 2 miles from Rancho Buena Vista and is at the lip of the wide arroyo along which the colony of San Bruno was established in 1683.

there is one Class IV rise just off the blacktop. From the rancho to the corral on the edge of the arroyo it is Class V and VI, requiring four-wheel-drive for the most part. We were locked-in and using compound low the entire distance because that track sees only horses and cattle.

The run to the rancho is 30 minutes from the blacktop; the run from the rancho to the corral or the beach is another 15 to 30 minutes.

MILE SAN BRUNO—THE OLD COLONY SITE

0 **Begin at kilometer 25 north of Loreto. The white road posts are marked. Right turn off Mex 1 when coming from Loreto.**

1.4 **Road forks, take either; they join ahead. Right in stream bed, left on bank.**

1.7 **Forks rejoin and climb out of stream bed.**

1.9 **Rancho El Paraiso. Road passes ranch house, turns right, circles around in wide arroyo, then curves back left to the east toward the sea.**

3.6 **Class IV down, short.**

4.2 **Alternate route in from Loreto joins here after coming from k 20.**

4.8 **Rancho Buena Vista. Large windmill, corral, and house. Straight ahead around rancho for Sea of Cortez 2 miles and area just south of Punta Mangles.**

To find track to corral proceed around ranch house and turn right as if going to beach. Within 100 feet a dim track will be visible in the grass to the left; it leads the 2 miles to the corral and south edge of the arroyo. If you follow this track for San Bruno site:

6.8 **Corral. Park, or if on bike, proceed through corral and down into arroyo. Then go left, west up arroyo, angling across to north side where the site of San Bruno is about 1 mile in.**

Expect Class II and III to rancho Buena
Vista.
Expect Class V and VI and to use 4WD from
rancho to corral.

LORETO

Loreto and its beaches: It all began here. True, La
Paz was the first landing of western explorers in
Baja—men of Cortez in 1534 in 1535 Cortez himself.
But it was at Loreto that the Jesuits in 1697 came
ashore with a mandate to do with Baja what they
could. Everything else having failed, the Spanish
crown saw fit to unleash the bold missionaries on the
dry peninsula. In their way they triumphed.

Here at Loreto was the first capital of both Baja
California and the present California of the United
States. And here the first mission, built in that same
year, still stands today. And from here, on a much
smaller scale but in a manner similar to the Romans,
the priests fanned out over the land, built roads,
connected 19 more missions to each other, and gave
Baja its first and one of its best administrative and
agricultural systems.

The system was later to decay, and the last mission
was closed in 1849. Today the few missions remaining intact are used by the local residents. And the
awful damage that disease visited upon Baja's more
than 50,000 native Indians in five major tribes, while
these missions were being founded, cannot go without mention.

At Loreto a portion of the mission has become a
fine museum run by the National Institute of History
and Anthropology. Don't miss it. Too many do.

I first saw Loreto from a Mexican bus and little
could have happened to discourage me more. The
small town of 3000 is slow and quiet and seemingly
in constant slumber. I wondered if anything *ever* happened. I found that Loreto is emerging from a long
sleep. Some have compared it to a South Seas island,
and I agree. There is a calmness and tranquillity

*The first mission, called Nuestra Senora de Loreto, is no
longer at this site and the present structure is the result of
several efforts over many years. It is, however, an impressive Baja landmark and is located in Loreto.*

about Loreto found nowhere else in Baja. Business is
done there, and all services are available, but no one
is in a hurry to display or advertise them. If you peek
and poke amidst the curtain of palms and bushy plants
you will find the stores and motels and cafes hidden
around corners and in the backs of homes.

South of Loreto begin the beaches to which the log
road following takes you. You can take as much or as
little time as you want to each; all are within a day's
round trip of Loreto.

LORETO TO NOPOLO, NOTRI, JUNCANLITO, PUERTO ESCONDIDO, LIGUI

MILE

0 Set your trip-gauge at 0 at the Loreto Pemex, just west of town on the road exiting
to Mex 1. Proceed west to Mex 1 and turn
left, south. Be very careful on this junket.
At 8 mile the turnoff marked by a sign that
says Nopolo on Mex 1 does not go there at
all.

5.9 Unmarked left turn off Mex 1 between
barbed-wire fencing and a gate which is
sometimes closed but not locked. You will

know this turnoff by its cobblestone road that goes straight to the water and then turns right to the beach; distance 2 miles. The road is the result of the intention of wealthy Loreto residents to make a resort of the fine bay. So far there is only the road and the almost always deserted bay. No services of any kind at Nopolo. There is good parking; it probably is private property, so one should use the road and beach with great care.

6.1 El Vivero experimental station on the right. Trees.

7.7 Right turn off Mex 1 to Rincon village.

8.0 False turn to Nopolo. A left turn here will take you to the beach, .5 of a mile, but a lagoon separates you from the main bay at Nopolo. This turn is worthwhile for a day's walk along the beach beneath the high rocks here and for some good fishing in the calm surf.

10.3 Notri. A fine view of the offshore islands, rocky beach, some access along a rocky road, Class III. Some small camping spots.

14.3 Excellent beach, some commercial development, but both north and south of this spot there are other beaches with greater privacy. The entry for them is here. You might have to pay $1 to get to them. No services. Class II road.

16.1 Puerto Escondido. Delightful landlocked bay. Fishing charters and food, but no gas or lodging available.

22.1 Ligui, rancho, deserted beach, fishermen's huts. Class III to this final beach before the road goes inland. Sierra de la Giganta mountains loom large over all these beaches.

Expect Class II and III sandy roads to each beach.

BEYOND PICHILINGUE

Northeast of La Paz: Pronounced peachy-leen-gay, this is the name of the little bay north of La Paz into which the Mazatlan ferry slips. Beyond this point, where the pavement ends, the surprises of La Paz begin. This 10-mile-wide peninsula jutting out and protecting La Paz Bay is usually forgotten in the rush to see the city of La Paz or to get south and do all the other things that come up in urban Baja.

The peninsula is like a miniature Baja with water on each side, clear bays, high cliffs, breakers, fishing, and excellent camping and beachcombing. Then why is no one there? I don't know. Perhaps the dirt roads discourage them; perhaps they go to other places. The roads are all Class II and III with short stretches of IV and V (these to view points off the main dirt roads).

On one trip to this area I watched the sleek white ferry make its smooth arrival between Tecolote Beach and Isla Ispiritu Santo—a fine sight. On another I watched from a high cliff as great, gray fish below me swam in large arcs in the clear blue-green waters.

This area is reached by driving to the ferry terminal 11 miles north of La Paz and following the dirt and gravel road over the little hill there and out into the flats and hills of the peninsula. The jewellike bay of Balandras (the name of a type of sailing vessel) awaits with unbelievably perfect symmetry; to its right the waters of El Tecolote stretch east around the point, while side roads lead often to beaches on which virtually no one is ever found.

It is an hour's drive from town to this exceptional area, most of which can be explored and enjoyed in a single day. It remains one of La Paz's least publicized recreation spots.

LA PAZ TO PICHILINGUE, BALANDRAS AND TECOLOTE

MILE

0 Set trip-gauge at 0 on Malecon, seawall at base of Cinco de Mayo Street and proceed toward ferry terminal at Pichilingue, north-northeast. On the right will be the La Paz residence of the President of Mexico. On the way the road will cut inland and pass a favorite city beach on the left, some oil storage tanks, in the hills and several little lagoons on the left as you near the ferry docks.

10.5 Alternate right turn for Balandras Bay, keep straight.

10.9 Ferry docks.

11.5 Pinchilingue Beach, commercialized.

12.5 Road left to beach, deserted bay, some parking, Class III and IV. 1 mile to beach.

12.8 Road left to beach, tiny bay, deserted, little parking, Class III and IV. 1 mile to beach.

13.5 Alternate route right to other side of peninsula, keep straight.

14.0 Laguna Azul surrounded by low, brushy mangrove, some mud. Keep left here for Balandras Bay and government monument. A walk up to the monument will reveal the beaches below. Hold onto your heartstrings.

15.7 Go right for loop over to Tecolote on the other side of peninsula. Not as nice as Balandras, more open. Go left here for rough road up to view point.

16.2 A second road goes left up to the view point. Very steep. Class V grade.

18.0 Big parking area, old rancho, beach ahead. Right turn goes to Tecolote, left stays in area.

18.2 Point and beach. Rocky, some sand, windy.

18.5 Road turns inland away from beach. Beach road straight ahead ends in deep sand. Road inland will fork to left for alternate return to La Paz. Not recommended.

20.2 You have wound slowly over the hills and back down to the intersection at 16.2 from town. Going back into La Paz the turnoffs are as follows:

20.5 Right turn for view point. 4WD only.

21.0 Right turn for Balandras Bay and monument.

35.0 Reach La Paz.

Expect Class II and III on all this route, except that on routes to beaches other than Balandras and El Tecolote, the rocky entrances will be Class IV and V with some VI.

LOS PLANES AND DEADMAN BAY

South of La Paz a good road climbs over the mountains, passes the high ranchos, and descends from the ridges on a straight, dusty incline to the valley and small farming community of Los Planes. Beyond Los Planes is a series of bays and beaches of white sands and rocky points that few tourists see.

The road out of La Paz, marked "Los Planes," is a two-hour run on 30 miles of graded Class I and II. At Los Planes there are no services or gasoline but there are food and refreshments at the grocery store.

Just before Los Planes one may turn left for El Sargento, on the north side of Ventana Bay, or continue to the southern, less-used section where Punta Arena (Norte) and the Punta Arena lighthouse are located. Here there are excellent opportunities for bird photography and good views of the big Isla Cerralvo 18 miles long, 5 miles wide, on which until the eighteenth century a large tribe of Indians flourished year-round.

Beyond Punta Arena is a tiny hidden bay, as yet unnamed, and beyond it, further around the point, the almost forgotten and almost perfectly round Deadman Bay. The bay received its name when an American attempt, in 1863, to colonize the bay failed and many

---

On the cut-off from Los Planes to San Antonio the dirt road often runs into the water-filled channel of the San Antonio River as it does here at mile 14.6

LOS PLANES AND DEADMAN BAY

of the colonists died. When we saw it in the afternoon, with the small rancho on one shore, a sleek multimasted South American yacht anchored in its center, and its long curving beach to the right, Deadman Bay imprinted an image on the mind that demanded a future return.

Expect Class II and III into the beaches near Los Planes and El Sargento. To loop out, rather than return to La Paz by the same route, turn right at mile 25.4 for the 15-mile, two hour trip to San Antonio as indicated on the following road log. However, this route is less suitable for a passenger auto; it is generally Class III in river arroyos right to the center of San Antonio, at which time the track climbs out of the river up onto the pavement of Mex 1.

LA PAZ TO LOS PLANES
AND DEADMAN BAY

MILE	
0	At turnoff for Los Planes 2 miles south of La Paz on Mex 1.
5.5	Road winds upward after passing over washboard surface.
10.5	Top ridge for good view to left of big mountains. Rock hounds will find loose quartz along top of this ridge.
15.3	Rancho La Huerto.
14.5	Tamales road to right, keep straight.
16.3	Rancho Las Encinitas.
16.5	View of Sea of Cortez and Bahia Ventana.
16.6	Begin down.
17.7	Rancho road right.
18.2	Deep gorge to right. Running water, falls. Ahead the road will cross a tiny running creek.
18.8	Canyon is now on left. Old structure across the canyon.
24.3	San Ignacio road to left, keep right.
25.4	San Antonio cutoff to right at large green shrine. From time to time there may be water in the riverbed that this road follows to San Antonio. Distance, 15 miles Class III with spots of IV.
28.1	Rancho to right.
28.6	First huts and outskirts of Los Planes. Go straight through town.
31.9	Ranchos on left of badly eroded route, irrigation acqueduct on left. Fork left, go straight, some signs may exist.
32.9	Sharp left for beaches and Punta Arena. Straight dead-ends.
35.1	Rancho left.
35.2	Rancho left.
36.6	Sharp left for Punta Arena, straight ahead 1.5 miles for Deadman Bay.
39.6	Straight ahead for Punta Arena, hidden bay .5 mile to right.
40.7	Rancho and salt ponds, Punta Arena and beach. Road dead-ends.

THE REMOTE LOOP

San José Del Cabo via Cabo Pulmo: The least-understood of Baja loops is this remote, difficult path along the extreme southern and eastern edge of the Sea of Cortez from Las Cuevas, on Mex 1 south of La Paz, to San José Del Cabo at the end of the peninsula. The coastline remains a wilderness.

The more I tried to find out about it, the more convinced I became no one really knew. One Mexican trucker stated flatly it was impossible; a fat American in a red jeep said it was a snap; most people didn't even know where it was. There was only one way to find out about it.

Reading the map, the traveler's eye is pulled toward this remote loop of coastal road as an alternate way to reach or return from Cabo San Lucas. It looks shorter and perhaps more interesting than the obvious loop back through Todos Santos. (See page 47.)

Keep in mind that neither of these loops is a Sunday

picnic. The traveler who believes he can slip down to "Cabo" from La Paz and then zip back through Todos Santos or the remote loop described here is wrong. The only quick and easy way back to La Paz from the end of the Baja Peninsula is Mex 1. The Remote Loop does begin on good Class II dirt road. But at Los Frailes, 30 miles in, it is strictly a four-wheel-drive affair.

However, the trip to Los Frailes and Cabo Pulmo alone is well worth the drive in. Neither place is often visited or well developed, and the bays and beaches are comparable to, if not better than, those south of Loreto. Because of the proximity of the Pacific Ocean the breakers are bigger than elsewhere in the Sea of Cortez, especially south of Punta Arena (Sur).

There are no services at either place; gas and food should be gained at La Ribera, 10 miles from Mex 1. If you do choose to tackle the entire Remote Loop, keep these facts in mind: It takes a full day from Las Cuevas to San José Del Cabo. If you haven't done it before, running it from north to south, as in this log, lessens the chances of getting lost. It is a 70-mile stretch—the first 30 easy, the middle 20 nearly impossible (except for a dune buggy), and the final 20 difficult. There are no services of any kind along the way.

There are a few tiny ranchos and many places for camping alone on a "private" beach. The people at one rancho beyond Los Frailes have become used to assisting bug-eyed travelers bogged down in sand and mumbling about the impossible mess the "road" is in.

Beyond Los Frailes the road is Class V and VI where there is rock and earth. But where there is not, where the road goes over sand dunes or into sandy arroyos near the ocean, it is Class VIII and IX, and for all but dune buggies a challenge with potential for failure.

I've done it in four-wheel-drive and on a motorcycle. But the Toyota's tires were quite deflated to improve traction; nevertheless, failure was a close companion all the way. On the Honda it was a matter of squirreling uphill in deep sand and more than once getting off, rear tire spewing sand, and with sweaty back wrestling it to the top. A companion vehicle is desirable. A single four-wheel-drive could easily bury all four-wheels.

But as with so many other parts of Baja which are hard to reach, the effort is repaid many times over by the free beaches and undisturbed country, and of course the adventure of besting a difficult opponent.

The beaches here are a combination of silver and gray sands, and because of the slightly heavier rainfall on the cape, they are laced with a bit more green, and palm trees grow at many.

The low mountains that roll up to the ocean are thick with forests of tall cactus and low brush. The inhabitants of the small ranchos along the way use the cactus for fencing and corrals. Horses and cattle are common if underfed.

Traveling this little-used loop you will probably not meet any other vehicles. The tracks you will pass over most often will be the hoofprints of cattle and horses. And where the road is less difficult, it is firm and smooth, with no holes or erosion. It is even enjoyable to negotiate as it winds up and down the low hills and valleys among cactus and tiny ranchos. But where the road is bad it is downright nasty and dangerous. How you choose to get your vehicle through those spots will depend on your knowledge, judgment, skill, and luck. On the Remote Loop all four will be often tested.

LAS CUEVAS TO SAN JOSÉ DEL CABO VIA CABO PULMO

MILE

0   Set trip-gauge at 0 at Las Cuevas junction on Mex 1 about 80 miles south of La Paz. Coming south you turn left to the coast; heading north, turn right. Sign indicates "La Ribera."

1.5   Road right, keep left and straight ahead. Fenced field on left.

3.3   Cattle-guard crossing, rough. Enter flat plain.

4.9   Cattle-guard crossing, rough. Continue straight across plain.

7.3 Dwellings of La Ribera right and left. Watch for sharp right ahead. Sea not visible.

7.5 Grocery store on right corner, church to left. (Buy any supplies you need in La Ribera. None are ahead.) Make sharp right to begin paralleling coast south. Pemex station is just ahead on right.

8.4 Pemex station. It is best to enter this stretch with full tanks.

16.5 Palms of La Laguna. Angle to right. Punta Arena lighthouse visible on sea. This is also the Tropic of Cancer. Road is Class II to this point and continues Class II with short portions of III and IV all the way to Los Frailes.

18.8 Planned community with fountain in center of road. Deserted except for Mexican Highway Maintenance crew.

20.7 Road left to beach .5 mile.

20.8 Road swings away from beach and begins climb up rocky ridge. Up .4.

21.2 Top. Dramatic view of coast north and south.

22.5 Bottom. Rancho and beach to left .5 mile.

24.0 Climb up ridge. Cabo Pulmos below and to the left. Several roads ahead go left to Cabo Pulmos beach area.

28.5 Rancho.

30.5 Top ridge for view of Los Frailes, large coastal rocks in distance. Begin long straight inland stretch.

31.5 Straight road begins to angle left toward the sea.

36.5 Return to sea. Mexican fishing camp populated by 50 fishermen.

37.2 Large Rancho La Boca Salado. Here road turns left into ranch yard, dwelling straight ahead, various fowl in yard, corral to left, horses and mules. The road seems to end at the front yard of the ranch, and in a way it does. Off to the right of the ranch, south and east, a track resembling a mule trail wanders away over rocks and boulders and through large cactus. Perhaps the foreman Miguel will be around and come out. He will eye your outfit critically as you ask him questions about the "road" ahead. When he finds out you intend to drive the road to San José Del Cabo he will shrug and murmur a quick prayer and probably advise you to turn around and drive back the way you came. When you leave La Boca Salado south you enter the roughest part of this loop.

The road leaves the rancho and immediately enters treacherous white sand. You will proceed up a small hill, within sight of everyone at the rancho, battling a trough of deep sand the whole way. Spewing sand and swearing you will wind up the hill through a narrow gauntlet and continue on fair road to a dropoff down the other side of the hill, in an equally bad narrow trough. Once down this hill you are committed to going all the way.

38.9 Down the dropoff the road will carry you to the much more modest Rancho Ardilla where there is a small corral and dwelling. They are a few hundred feet back from the white sands and catch the shade of a palm tree grove. The family, barefoot, will peek curiously and the owner will walk out to greet you. It is hard not to halt at each of these lonely ranchos, not only to verify where you are, but because of the feeling it would be impolite not to. Tough, short upgrade.

40.7 Here you get into truly isolated, deserted white beaches just off the road and over the dunes. How you reach and use them will depend on your gear and the amount of time you can spend. Getting off the narrow road to the beaches, or just to park, means tangling with the cactus. This first of the remote beaches is a fine one.

42.1　Beach. 42.5, beach; 42.6, beach.

42.7　Long, wide sandy beach, shading palms, apparently deserted old rancho, last really bad section of deep sand.

44.8　Turn slowly into mountains, leave beaches, canyon to right with dwelling down old road, 4WD not essential after this.

46.4　Small, clean rancho, corral of cactus; pigs, fowl, cattle.

48.0　Top summit. Cactus so close to road they seem to challenge the way.

49.1　*Major Intersection*: The road you are on ends at T intersection. The road right winds 7 miles to a small rancho and ends. The road left, the one you want, drops down and over a little rock culvert. The high peaks of the Sierra De La Laguna appear to the right. Mex 1 is between them and the road you are on.

50.1　The road has been very confusing twisting and turning. It even begins to disappear, but bear with it. It will drop into an old riverbed of white sand, brush, rocks, and trees, and at one point on the left an old elephant tree struggling with drought, wind, and earth has grown into the side of a giant boulder.

53.4　Road begins to look like it is going somewhere and is joined by a road coming in from the right. Keep straight ahead. The earth is now red and gravel surfaced. More ranchos appear.

64.7　Arrive at community of Catarina, a school at hilltop on left, homes on right and left, the main road is the one most traveled.

64.9　You are in the center of Catarina, to the right is a school with a fenced playground. At this school you must turn right. The road goes west toward Mex 1 and the jagged mountains.

65.6　After traveling west about a half-mile you will come to a T intersection. Go left past a pumping station on the left. Just beyond it bear hard right, again west toward the mountains.

66.4　Blacktop just north of Santa Anita and 8 miles north of San José Del Cabo. Turn left for San José Del Cabo, right for La Paz.

Expect Class II and III in beginning from Las Cuevas.

Expect Class VII and VIII with some IX from Los Frailes.

Expect Class III and IV with some V from mile 44.8.

See page 49 for additional roads in this area.

4

BETWEEN FRIENDS

"Why anyone would ever want to go Baja I'll never know!"
Anonymous tourist returning to U.S. border, 1976.

"But I saw the earth at peace, at peace the heavens, blue the mountain and the wind at rest."
Enrigue Gonzales Martinez,
Wring the Swan's Neck, 1942.

"Each year the lure of rutted roads winding through the desert country draws me with an irresistible force. . . . Each time I penetrate the unknown I find my appetite for further adventure is whetted to a point where I feel I must return with more elaborate preparations and better equipment to penetrate a little deeper yet."

Erle Stanley Gardner,
The Hidden Heart of Baja, 1962.

"There, souls explode like the colors and voices and emotions. The important thing is to go out, to open a way, get drunk on noise, people, colors. And this fiesta, shot through with lightning and delirium, is the brilliant reverse to our silence and apathy, our reticence and gloom."

Octavio Paz,
*The Labyrinth of Solitude:
Life and Thought in Mexico*, 1959.

BETWEEN FRIENDS

The following bits of information might now and then be found helpful as you roll southward deeper into the mysteries, adventures, and endless beauties of Baja California.

You can order "frijoles, tortillas, and coffee" almost anywhere and anytime of day or night in Baja for 10 pesos. It's a good, cheap, snack to know about —particularly since, within reason, the hot tortillas will keep coming as long as you need more.

In Mexico *each cup of coffee is a separate production*. If you ask for a refill a new cup will be delivered and charged for.

If you want real coffee instead of the cup of hot water and instant Nescafe from a jar that you will almost always find there, ask for "Cafe du grano" and you will get brewed coffee if someone has the time to make it.

Watch out for the Nescafe. It's strong. Use a half-teaspoon with that cup of water or you will have wasted your money.

Coffee in Baja is five, six, or seven pesos, depending on where you are, and so your cheapest single cup is going to cost about 25¢.

The long peninsula holds for each its special pleasures and attractions.

The most exquisite cup of coffee in all of Baja is found in La Paz at an open-air coffee counter, called "Cafe Battala," on Francisco I. Madero Street, one block to the right of the main plaza coming from the Malecon. The beans are ground each morning, and the coffee is only one peso. There are no chairs.

Most laundromats (called lavamaticas) use American coins and have instructions in English. A few use pesos, and none are any great hurdle. Ask for help; there is always sign language.

Carry your own camera film to Baja. No one is going to check the amount you take in, unless it is beyond all reason. If you do run out, both color and black-and-white are available, but in very limited variety, particularly black-and-white. Any film you can find between Ensenada and La Paz will cost *twice* its stateside price. A roll of 36-frame Kodachrome 64 sells in La Paz for more than $5 American. If you can find black-and-white it will be Plus-X, and it is often very old. I have found film in tiny quantities in the following towns: Guerrero Negro, San Ignacio, Santa Rosalia, Mulege, Loreto, and Ciudad Constitucion.

Adventure in Baja sometimes means a ferry ride. These are the approximate routes and times at Baja's three ferry ports: three days a week from Santa Rosalia to Guaymas, leaving at night for a 10-hour crossing; daily from La Paz to Mazatlan, leaving in the afternoon for a 12-hour crossing; daily from Cabo San Lucas to Puerto Vallarta, leaving in the afternoon for a 14-hour crossing. No ferries connect Baja ports only. They are modern, large, clean ships, and the Sea of Cortez is generally calm.

Ferry fares vary with the ports but passenger only to the mainland will run $10 or less, an auto around $40 or less.

Be careful boarding a ferry. Remove what you want from your auto before you drive on. Only *one person* is allowed in the auto driving on, and once underway no one is allowed below decks.

The ferries have showers and most of the foot passengers, to no one's embarrassment, sleep on the floor of the modern lounge or on the rear deck.

Want to call home? The telephone company in Baja prefers you to make the call collect. That's *por corbrar*. Look for a blue and white *Larga Distancia* sign. In La Paz it's in the ice cream parlor off the main square, in San Quintin in the City Hall, in Colonia Guerrero in the single gas station, and in other towns in other restaurants and businesses. If you write down the number and the city and state, *your* name, and the words *por corbrar*, the call will usually go through quickly. Do not expect bilingual operators.

Although the call itself will go through quickly there is usually a line at any long-distance phone in Baja. Better bring a book. For person-to-person just write additional words, *persona-a-persona*. If you don't do this, the assumption is that you will talk to anyone who answers, including your 3-year-old nephew.

Need money wired? Have a friend send it to *your name* via Western Union to the National Telegraph System. Western Union will know how to do it. But you will have to be in a *major city* to receive it. It will arrive in Baja within hours after it is wired from the States, but it will take two or three days for your name to appear on the administrative list for payment. You don't have to tell the Baja office anything beforehand; the money will come to them automatically. When your name appears on the list (it is published twice each weekday, once on Saturday, and not at all on Sunday) you identify yourself and claim the money. You will be paid there in pesos. The charge to you will be about 50¢ and the charge in the States to the sender several dollars.

If you decide to send a wire *out* of Baja California the cost for 15 words, which can be English, is $5. This cost varies little between La Paz and Ensenada. For the same price a night letter containing 50 words may be sent. Depending on when your telegram is sent 10 to 12 hour service or less may be expected.

Plan on getting mail in Baja? The delay in smaller towns may be as much as 7 days, in larger towns less. The General Delivery system in Baja, as on the mainland, is different than that you are used to in the States.

Have your mail addressed to your name care of *La*

Lista and the name of the town and state in Mexico. There are no corresponding ZIP codes. Each day a list is prominently posted in the post office or is held by a clerk. It is in alphabetical order and remains up for several days, but the mail will be held longer, about 30 days. However, mail addressed to me was once held for a year, but this was in the grocery store–post office of a small village. The envelopes spent their 12 months, along with other gringo mail, in a bin of red beans.

Cows will kill you. If you drive at night in Baja you will eventually collide with a dumb Mexican cow. The day will come when one will slowly wander in front of you. No beast cares less about highways and autos than a Mexican cow or steer.

Some, startled on one side of the road, will run across to the other side of the road to get away from an oncoming auto. Burros, mules, and donkeys run a close second. I once came suddenly upon a little burro seeking food on the center line. I didn't know which way he intended to jump so I slowed way down while he made up his mind. Finally I had to halt within a few inches of his rear. He turned and brayed loudly in my face and then walked slowly off the pavement. Be ready to meet animals anywhere, anytime, on Mexican roads.

If you are tired of beer or American soft drinks, a welcome change you might want to try is Vita-Limon, a Mexican product, or the many juices that come in cans.

To get a higher octane gasoline than available at the Pemex stations, find out which airports are close to the highway and buy aviation gas at a slightly higher but not exorbitant price. Arnold Senterfitt's definitive book *Airports of Baja* is an aid.

There are two kinds of gasoline at Pemex Stations: Nova, which is leaded but low octane, and Extra, which is a higher octane (said to be about equal to stateside regular) but unleaded. Many drivers mix the two to get both the lead and the higher octane. I've tried Nova alone and don't hold much hope for it; the pinging and power loss are really bad. On the other hand, the mixture seems to work well. Extra costs a bit more, 4 pesos a liter rather than 3, but it is worth the price. Gas stations often run out of Extra and have only Nova, because Mexican customers prefer Extra.

The favorite Mexican swear word is cabron, *meaning cuckold.* It is used much like SOB in the States. You will hear it not once, but several times each day —probably, however, not directed at yourself. The word "gringo," invested with the proper angry tone, seems able to carry the meaning of any swear word. But don't let it offend you; it is used in many ways, and often in good humor.

A personal check is not usually acceptable payment for goods or lodging unless you know the people. Mexico has its own credit card system, but many motels and other businesses will accept Master Charge and American Express. But find out the price *before* you indicate payment will be by plastic. A 50¢ increase is reasonable, several dollars is not.

When you ask directions in Baja some people will give distances in miles (mee-lays) but almost always the answer will be in kilometers (kee-low-meetrows), so you should have some system of your own for converting them to miles.

When you buy gasoline forget the credit card you are accustomed to. All gasoline in Baja is sold for cash only. If you speak little Spanish one way to ask for gas is to name an amount in pesos, for instance, "50 pesos por favor." Find out how many pesos' worth your tank holds.

I've been to Baja many ways and my dress has run the gamut. How you are treated will generally vary with your dress and with whom you are dealing. But the real determinant is not your dress but in whether or not you are able yourself to act courteously and with humility, no matter what the circumstance.

Once, in 1974, I was walking along outside Santa Rosalia. I suppose I was rather shabby looking—sunburnt, a pack on my back, an old fedora atop long hair. The federales halted me and demanded my papers, which I produced. It was a Mutt and Jeff routine, with the little cop acting nice and the big one with gold teeth glowering at me the whole time. I had heard enough horror stories to be concerned.

"So, you are a heepy," the little one said, returning my papers. "We doan like heepies," he smiled at me.

"What would you like me to do?" I asked. I had a letter in my pocket with seals and so forth but didn't wish to bring it out.

"We doan wan you heech-hiking. You got no money?"

I told them I did.

"We take you to town then and you ride the bus."

I rode the bus.

No one has ever torn my pack apart or insulted me. Indeed, the federales have helped me on with the pack and been open and generous with help and advice.

There have been exceptions. Riding one black midnight on the purple Las Tres Estrellas Del Oro express from La Paz to Tijuana, my wife Mary and I were jolted awake suddenly when the bus stopped quickly for red flares.

We were boarded immediately by one man who menaced us knowingly with his stubby automatic rifle. He looked like a recent escapee from a mental hospital. His crossed eyes were heavy with hate and his handling of the weapon was fearsome.

He spoke no English and since Mary and I were in the first seat he hissed at me, "Arriba pronto! Y manos arriba!" and pointed the weapon at me. "Donde va, eh? Donde es tu marijuana?" He felt my pockets full of film. Grinning and stepping away he ordered, "Sientese!" And went on down the aisle, intimidating other passengers at random.

A second man boarded holding a 45 automatic pistol and in English asked if we had any luggage. Determining we did he ordered us both off into the desert and along with us several Mexican passengers.

The man with the rifle stood to the side while suitcases were examined. Ours were never sought and everyone was loaded back on the bus.

This happened just north of Guerrero Negro. Later in the year a motel owner with whom I was talking there recalled the few days the examinations were being made. He said the worst part of it was that the men were "sin uniformas," without uniforms, and I had to agree with him.

Don't carry drugs or other contraband into Mexico. There is nothing there to protect you from your own stupidity. Know the laws before you go and intend to obey them. Don't break the law while you are there—not for fun, not for *any* reason.

The foundation of Mexican law is not the Anglo-Saxon system we are used to but the Roman system. One of its vestiges is that in Mexico, until you are proven innocent, you are guilty.

If you have a breakdown in Mexico the chances are good that a repairman is near. There is an equally good chance the repairman will come to your vehicle rather than it to him. Don't be surprised to see engines being rebuilt at various places along the highways and dirt roads, another parallel between Baja and Alaska.

If Baja was not the birthplace of the saying "There is more than one way to skin a cat," it is certainly living proof of the old maxim. Baja mechanics, one finally comes to believe, can fix anything. However, they curse and are often mystified as are their American counterparts, by the pollution control equipment that now entangles so many American auto engines.

In 1958, in Ensenada, the universal joint of my Isetta 300 went out, and while I sat for three days playing chess in the front yard of Fauftimo Sandoval's "Transmissiones Automaticas," Fauftimo and his two sons fabricated a new part out of sheet metal, inner tubes, and cardboard, all the while feeding and sleeping my brother and me on their dirt floor. The final price was named when Fauftimo grasped a stick and in the sand in front of his garage drew a $ sign next to a 1 and a 0, and then cocked his eyes up at me. We had $11. We gave Fauftimo 10 of them and left Baja. The part lasted to Los Angeles and that was fine with us.

Banditos? Is there any real danger in Baja? No—no more so than traveling in California. Items appear in newspapers about tourists being harmed or killed in Mexico. The same events are reported about New York, and tourists keep going there. But if it happens in Mexico, and to an American tourist, then it is given some extraordinary meaning, and Americans start wishing Teddy Roosevelt were around with his big stick.

What about fake roadblocks and the danger of remote areas? The fake roadblock is one of Mexico's wildest rumors, one that gives so much joy in the telling that it is guaranteed long life. And as for being robbed in a remote area of Baja, the foolish would-be assailant would probably die of old age waiting on Baja's offbeat back roads for enough gringos to come along to support him.

Logic insists that a tourist is safer in the remote areas than in the cities, particularly in Baja. Life in the United States has already made that fairly plain.

If you use common sense in selecting a site for your tent or camp, nothing will be stolen from it. Almost every bust and theft I have heard about was a result of an American's foolishness.

And theft from motel rooms simply does not occur. Isolated incidents will happen, of course, just as they do in the States. But the wise motel patron does not leave valuables lying about as a test for kleptomania. The test might prove positive.

Anything I have lost through theft in Baja I would have lost in the States. Afterall, when I returned to the La Paz bus station, did I really expect to find the portable typewriter I had left sitting on the bench two hours before?

In spite of stories blown out of proportion, and almost always without full details, Mexico is as safe to travel as the United States, perhaps safer.

It is true that the American tourist is down off the pedestal, but isn't that now true everywhere? And it is true that in certain parts of Mexico where criminal activity—particularly drug smuggling—is high, and where Americans are involved, some Americans are getting killed. But there are certain parts of America, particularly in the big cities, where a Mexican or European tourist wouldn't last an hour.

No one denies that some Americans have been senselessly killed in Mexico and that others have been purposely robbed, but these incidents, as sad and serious as they are, in no way reflect the general condition in that country, particularly not in Baja. Banditos? Practically none. The danger of robbery or theft? So low as to be almost nonexistent. Relax and enjoy your travels in Baja. You will find the people there as good as or better than the people you know here.

THE MOTORCYCLE IN BAJA

There is so much myth and misunderstanding about two-wheeling down this stretch of wild land south of California that even bikers become confused when they start thinking about going.

This part is not about the dirt racing that goes on down there, from Ocotillo to Ojos Negros and on new and old courses further south. That is a pursuit separate from touring and exploring.

Everybody worries about getting his bike stolen. The first time I went to Baja on a bike I hauled down 20 pounds of chains and locks and slept with a rope tied between my bike and my foot. I had been assured my bike would be stolen the moment it was out of my sight.

I don't do that anymore. I don't even carry a lock and chain, and since that first penetration it's been 20,000 theft-free bike miles in Baja. I had to go to L.A. to get my tool kit removed. But on the other hand I don't leave the key in the switch, and I always park the bike as if someone were going to try to steal it. I do the same in the States—and that's the point. Your bike can get stolen anywhere if you are careless, and probably won't be if you are not. The further you are from the big towns, the less the danger.

If you choose to go down Baja and not leave the blacktop, keep a few things in mind. Plenty of BMWs, Goldwings, and Moto-Guzzis make the trip every year, not to mention the Electra-Glides. They have a good time, see plenty of beaches, mountains, and good touring country, and never go in the dirt.

Some even head a mile or two up the back roads to camp a night and they don't encounter trouble. And when they pull up alone or in crowds in front of a motel they are welcome. There is no discrimination in Baja against bikers with the sole exceptions of the raucous northern beach town of San Felipe and one beach on Concepcion Bay. San Felipe and Concepcion Bay are a center of dune buggy and dirt-bike activity and some of the motels have decided to penalize all bikes, muffled or not.

So, if you're going to tackle the 2000 mile loop down to Cabo San Lucas and back, or any shorter

A motorcyclist in Baja checks his road map on the journey to Laguna Hanson.

A Compton, California, BMW group solved the problem in its own way. The group toured Baja followed by a two-ton van loaded with American gasoline and BMW parts and supplies.

The blacktop is good road all the way, but *it is not American freeway*, or even what we would call a high-speed two-lane road. There is no equivalent to a Highway Patrol or State Troopers. Speed limits, posted in kilometers, range from 50 to 80 mph.

Watch those Mexican curves! They possess what an irate biker-engineer described to me as "decreasing-radial-entries" which means they get sharper rather than easier as you roll into them. After stateside highways this takes getting used to.

Watch those Mexican shoulders. Or rather, their absence! We get spoiled in the States. Once, at day's end, near San Agustin, I lapsed for one short instant and flew into space at 75 mph down a 10-foot embankment, took a terrific helmet-smacking bounce against the windshield, burst on through cactus and big rocks and skidded back onto the blacktop without dropping more than 2000 rpm. I was lucky. I only looked away for a moment, but on the shoulderless Mexican roads, that's all it takes.

Watch those Mexican trucks and buses. They know you don't have a chance. And of course Mexican truckers and busdrivers have an enormous reputation to live up to, and scattering a motorcyclist over the desert could add something to it. Here's an example: I was moving one day at a comfortable 70 mph east over the pavement of Mex 2, a fairly well-maintained two-lanes between Mexicali and Tijuana, daydreaming in the May heat when far ahead I saw a big truck pull out to pass. It was coming at me.

My headlight was on; I had a white fairing: The driver would see me. He would pull in ahead of someone else in the long line of vehicles coming toward me. I knew all those things as I roared toward him at more than a mile a minute. Suddenly it was getting to be a very big truck.

The driver didn't bat an eye. He didn't signal me with his lights. He didn't even blow his horn. He barreled down my side of the road right for me at 80 mph—a huge KW tractor pulling a semi, the cab all

round trip, keep some of these tips in mind. The first several apply to any motorcycle in Baja, the later apply more to getting off the pavement.

The gasoline is not good, but it will work. The leaded is low octane, the unleaded high octane. Most riders mix the two. There is no reason for any engine damage to occur, although spark plugs may foul 10% to 20% sooner and there can be a very slight power loss. Oil is for sale everywhere.

Motorcycle dealers are all but nonexistent south of the border. After Ensenada the next is in La Paz where there are two small shops, each ready to be helpful but with extremely limited parts.

tassled and sainted—and never admitted by motion or eye-contact I was anywhere in Baja. He was going to pass that long line of slower-moving traffic (50 to 60 mph), and one motorcycle was expendable.

I hit the dirt and was back up on the highway without losing much speed, preferring chicken status to being ground-up in his radiator. As soon as it was over I wasn't sure it had happened. There hadn't even been any malice. I wasn't even worth *that*. It was then I began to shake.

If a bus gets behind you and wants by, pull over. And if a bus gets behind you without your knowing it and passes and pulls in you will be able to write your name in the dirt on its side.

For them it is a monotony-breaking game, a challenge—almost a duty—and certainly a way of life.

All publications tell you the insurance in Mexico is all the same. That is not true. Some companies will sell you full coverage on your bike and others will sell you only liability. And the rates do vary. With one company I paid $2 a day for liability only and that was a reduction for buying 60 days at a time; with another company I paid $1.76 a day for full coverage, including theft and collision, for any number of days.

Any insurance you may have purchased in the States is void in Mexico. If you have an accident in Mexico and do not have insurance you sit in jail until liability is determined and those injured have been compensated. If you have an accident in Mexico and there has been serious bodily injury or damage, *to anyone*, and you do have insurance, you sit in jail until proof of insurance is established through administrative channels, and then you are released. The Mexican police don't listen to all the b.s. at the scene. They take everyone to jail and then decide who was at fault. That's when you are really happy you purchased that expensive insurance policy. (And all short-term insurance has to be expensive because of the economics involved.)

You may choose to trailer, truck, or ride a bike down Baja to get off the blacktop and into the back country.

Heat is no problem, first because the bikes are built to take it and second because Baja, with the exception of the Mexicali triangle, just doesn't get that hot.

A doctor's wife sitting in an El Presidente restaurant looked at my light road bike one winter and said: "Do you just take off into the cactus?" It doesn't happen that way in Baja. You stay on the roads and trails because the surface of the rocky cactus-filled desert is not negotiable.

To give you some idea of what will go up and down most of Baja's back-country roads, I have used a 75 Honda CB 360cc road bike, which weighs 350 pounds dry, and I had plenty of extra weight on it. I have taken this bike at least once on almost every road in this book and was able to force, pull, kick, and shove it over the worst spots, including the Class X sections at Santa Maria. But I would never go in there again on such a bike; I came very close to having to leave it out there in the cactus and rock. I can't see doing these roads on anything mucher heavier than a 400cc. I'm six feet and weigh 170.

I have also used a 76 Honda XL 350 dirt bike, which took me with greater ease down some of Baja's meanest roads and up some of the more terrifying rocky grades with its fantastic top-end climb power at low rpm.

But the truth is: There are so few really bad spots in Baja that an investment of $1400 for an XL is not the best choice if you have to compromise. If you're going to trailer or truck it down, fine. But if you have to ride your bike to Baja, the road bike modified with knobbies or universals on front and rear and washable filters is the best choice. That's because the road bikes, in the end, do better off the road than the dirt bikes do on the road. And unless you are trailering, you will be biking as much *on* the pavement as off it. There's no avoiding it.

So, if you don't go down on anything bigger, how will you do on something smaller? It depends on how fast you want to go and how much you want to carry. A 100cc will get you up some of these steep grades, but you won't carry anything but yourself.

The smaller bikes' advantage of greater gas mileage is nice, for if you tour seriously on the back roads you will soon run up against the gas problem. I hauled a two-gallon can of gas on the back of my bike all over Baja. I rarely had use for it, but my range at 50 miles to the gallon was restricted without an over-sized tank. A one-gallon can is the better choice, but don't fill it until you know you are really going to need it. However, hauling any gas is a pain, so if you can convert to a larger tank, do so. A range of over 100 miles is rarely needed.

You will get flat tires, if not from nails then from cactus spines. Carry a pair of good long-nosed pliers to pull out the needlelike spines. Before you leave fill each tire with a half-bottle of no-flat. Carry with you two or more of the $5 pressurized spray-cans of flat repair and air.

Be prepared to fix your own flats. If you haven't done it before, do not go off-road in Baja without first pulling your wheel and tire off the bike, fixing a simulated flat, and then putting it back on. This is a must.

I prefer hot patches to the popular new cold patch-es, which never seem to bind just right. I like to see the flame and imagine the fine, secure weld resulting from it.

Do not go into the dirt in Baja without several cans of chain lube. I carry one can for every 500 dirt miles I expect to cover. Keeping the chain oiled is easier than trying to repair it. In unusually dusty or sandy stretches I oil at every stop. Keep it wet, keep it clean.

Adjust your chain once a day. The beating it takes out in the rocks and dirt requires it and will prolong its useful life.

Change your oil every 500 miles. If that seems extravagant, don't let it bother you. Just do it. It's inexpensive, it's easy, and it's one of the best things you can do to take care of an iron horse that is faith-fully carrying you over a very hot and hostile land that without your mount, could easily kill you.

Carry water. And carry as much as you can. Load requirements have priorities. You may never use it, but please take it with you. The day you really need it is the day it will save your life.

Get your dealer to supply you with some levers, spark plugs, points, and assorted nuts and bolts. And be sure to take your ratchet set. Sometimes the factory kit won't even allow you to get the drain plug out.

When night falls in the city and you want to leave your bike, here are some motels to know about where there are closed, secure courtyards in which your bike can be safely left while you eat dinner elsewhere. From north to south they are:

Motel San Quintin, San Quintin, $5 per night for a single. Hot water; security guard; mobile trailer units; bike parking in front of room.

Motel Baja Sur, Guerrero Negro, $7 per night for a double. Hot water; Carlos Garciglia, manager, speaks English; bikes welcome, secure parking in courtyard in front of room.

Posada Fischer, San Ignacio, $10 per night for a double. Hot water; Oscar Fischer, Jr., owner, speaks some English; bikes okay, secure parking in court in front of room. Half-mile from center of San Ignacio.

Hotel Central, Santa Rosalia, $2 per night for a single. Bathroom and shower in the hall; no English spoken; bikes okay in courtyard just across from main square, single bike can wheel into entryway next to restaurant for night security.

Junipero Serra, Loreto, $6 per night for a double. Hot water; Aurelio Robinson, owner; bikes okay, secure next to wall or in Aurelio's front yard for the night.

Hotel Mirabel, Ciudad Constitucion, $8 per night for a double. Hot water; credit cards accepted; bikes okay, one or two bikes may be wheeled right through hotel door off street into interior patio provided it's not leaking oil and you don't mind making a scene.

Hotel Yeneka, La Paz, $7 per night for a double. Hot water; Miguel Macias, owner; some English, boarder Al Sanchez teaches English in La Paz; court-yard locked at night, secure spot for one or two bikes. Located in the center of La Paz.

El Cardon, La Paz, $1 per night per person to pitch tent; more for auto; good clean trailer park with separators and hot showers. 3 miles north of La Paz.

Hotel Mi Rancho, Cabo San Lucas, $8 per night for double. Hot water; bikes okay, secure courtyard at night.

Of course, when you are offbeat there is no need to worry about your bike. However, there are a few other places to keep in mind where bikes are welcome: Mike's Sky Rancho; Laguna Hanson (cabins); Santa Ines Rancho at Cataviña (just south of the big new El Presidente there) where you can rent a bunk for the night for a dollar or two and not worry about your equipment; and of course the various missions in the back country.

Bikers are welcome, too, at the string of modern, expensive El Presidente motels, a partially government-subsidized operation to encourage tourism. And some of them have little courtyards here and there to tuck away a bike. If only they had hot water. The time may come when you will have no choice but an El Presidente and in spite of their intimidating atmosphere they manage friendliness and do accept credit cards for both the room *and* the food. So if you get down to plastic the El Presidentes are a way to get home.

No matter which way you use your bike in Baja, on the road or off, the chances are excellent that you will have a memorable trip and want to return again. Baja has that effect, and particularly on bikers. The lack of rain, the open country, the relaxed air make bike touring there a real pleasure.

Either way, set yourself up with a soft seat! I used a piece of foam rubber from a southern California surplus store and it saved my day. And custom seats can be purchased on either side of the border for $50 to $150.

About traveling light and food: At the end of one 43-day trip I wound up riding with a BMW owner out of Vancouver, B.C., who prepared himself a hot meal every morning and every night with a tiny stove and cook kit he carried on his 500cc bike. If you are going to be out six months, as he had been, that is the thing to do. But for a few days, or even a month, I don't think the extra weight is worth it.

Finally, if you are wondering whether you or your group will be okay at night in the desert with nothing but your head against your tire and your back to the heavens, the answer is yes.

I carried a poncho and medium sleeping bag and when the sun started saying good-bye for the day I *stopped early* and arranged a tiny camp, performed whatever maintenance the bike required (there was *always* something), used whatever food or water I happened to have to satisfy hunger and thirst, fixed the poncho next to the bike, used the foam seat for a pillow, rolled out the bag, dropped a Mexican wool blanket over it, and fell nightly into exhausted and undisturbed sleep. I never had a problem with snakes, scorpions, spiders, or flying or crawling insects, but then I was always careful, whenever able, to pick a site that would avoid such problems.

Alone in the desert I never built a fire. Somehow, particularly with the bright stars and tremendous full moons, a fire seemed unnecessary, and the stillness and the night became that much more meaningful.

A rule of thumb on finding a spot that is better than others is to pick one away from towns, ranchos, and as far from the roadway as possible. Another hint is to get yourself out of sight so you don't invite hurled objects and honking horns. When you have solved the "people problem" the next is terrain. Look first and see where the ants are at work so you don't lay your bag on top of their hill; keep away from rocks that snakes and dry wood scorpions may be using for homes. Pick a place where mist won't settle on you; a high spot. Most of all pick your spot of earth *before* the sun goes down. With daylight you can use judgment in selecting the right patch of sand or rocks to lay your head. At night it is all luck and only the foolish make camp in the wilds after the sun has gone down.

As to traveling light, the key question is whether or not you will eat in cafes or carry your own, and whether or not you will sleep out often (and therefore carry a tent and better bag and pad) or use hotels and motels. Once you have answered that question the gear you need is pretty obvious and the only questions are ones of degree. If you do opt for light traveling carry at least a cup for water and a single bowl and spoon for food. That's in case a fellow traveler makes a generous offer. And going light for sleeping would require at a minimum a light bag, ground cloth and blanket.

So there it is: biking Baja, the long open road stretching those thousand miles south with the promise of adventure, the golden beaches, the blue-green waters, the warm cape, the stars so brilliant at night, the dawns so clear with sharp, bold shadows. It is all there, waiting.

The Motorcycle Take-List
1. Poncho or other suitable ground-cloth.
2. Medium sleeping bag, down bag not required.
3. One wool blanket (optional).
4. Cup, plastic bowl (plastic wipes clean easier), knife, spoon.
5. Toothbrush, Lava soap, good towel for cleaning up.
6. At least one change of jeans (while the others are at laundromat).
7. Extra clothing and socks (amount optional).
8. Sun glasses, suitable face shield, and, if you wear glasses, a spare pair.
9. Good pair of gloves and spare pair.
10. Stout boots. (Get them shined often, about 5 pesos in the towns along the way.)
11. Helmet and alternate headgear (to protect head from sun if you have to walk out).
12. More than one map of Baja. (One will wear out with use.)
13. Sun tan lotion, chapstick. (Don't laugh—you're in the desert.)
14. Two water bottles or two canteens, filled. (Two because inevitably you will set one down somewhere and forget it.)
15. If available, an oversized fuel tank; if not, a one-gallon spare can filled only when you know you will need it.
16. For dirt roads change street tires to universals, rear to knobby if you're serious.
17. Following spare parts:
    1. 2 sets of spark plugs.
    2. washable filter for air cleaner. (You're in trouble in the dirt without one.)
    3. crankcase drain plug and gasket.
    4. brake and clutch handles, shift lever. (When you drop, these break.)
    5. miscellaneous nuts and bolts—your choice.
18. Wire, duc tape, rope, nylon cord.
19. A ratchet and socket set reduced to what you need plus good additional tools. In Baja do not depend on your factory tool kit, please!
20. Tire changing tools, tire patches, good working rags.
21. Soft seat.
22. First-aid and snake-bite kits.
23. An *extra key* for the *bike*.
24. If you don't smoke, matches.
25. *Chain lube*, plenty of it.
26. One or more cans of pressurized air and *No-Flat in each tire*.
27. Chain repair kit.
28. Personal items optional such as tent, additional food, cameras. Don't load yourself down. It is dangerous and will spoil the trip. Take less luggage and more money: the secret to a successful biking trip.

THE FOUR-WHEEL-DRIVE IN BAJA

The off-roader considering a trip to Baja gets conflicting accounts of what to expect and how to cope with it. This is not so much because the kind of four-wheeling down there is all that varied, but rather because so many people have their own personal preconceptions of what *must be there*, and what it must be like.

The fact that no one disputes, yet so few mention, is that the four-wheel-driver adventuring in Baja California is almost always going to be on dirt tracks already pioneered by Mexicans in pickup trucks. Unlike much of the Sierra-Nevada and the states of Nevada, Arizona, and New Mexico, where four-wheel driving is often over trails or solid granite or open desert where no vehicles, or at very best few,

This 1970 Toyota FJ-55 Four-Wheel Drive Station Wagon performed well in Baja, its sports Parnelli Jones rims and Concorde "Deserters" turned inside out to protect the lettering.

have ever been before, most of Baja's four-wheel-drive trails already function as Mexican "roads."

Because Baja is a narrow peninsula, and just about every part of it supports someone—a working rancho, a mine, or a fishing camp—Mexicans are always in motion, in and out of the mountains and along the beaches, in their cast-off American pickups. And what Mexicans can make these indomitable, battered old machines do must be seen to be believed. I won't

even try to describe it; no one would believe me. So there's no loss of pride or thrill in going where a Mexican pickup has already been.

Of course, there are places in Baja without roads, which four-wheel-drive vehicles can partially penetrate. But about the canyons and salt flats that seem accessible by four-wheel-drive but into which no track now leads, the best advice you will ever get is to *stay away*. If you are with someone else who has been in and come out again and knows his way around, fine. But I think most drivers will find that the known trails of Baja are going to offer them about all the excitement, danger, and reward they will be able to stomach in one lifetime.

Since Baja is a narrow strip of land, you are never too far from gasoline. But the rule remains: Fill up when you can. In Baja, stations do run out of gasoline. On the other hand, because of the almost constant proximity of gas supplies, two jerry-cans or one 10 gallon auxillary tank will be enough for most efforts. Of course, if you have a convenient way to carry more gas, then do it. If weight is no problem, it never hurts to have a lot more gas than you need.

Do not venture off the road anywhere in Baja without a minimum of five gallons of water per person in your vehicle. You will not use that much on the way, but if you break down it will sustain your life until help arrives. Since almost all of Baja's offbeat roads also serve practical functions someone comes along most of them at least once a day. So if you break down don't leave your vehicle. Of course, if you are on a track that has obviously not been used for a year or more, make your plans carefully, spend a day waiting for the unexpected, and then start out. Make sure you are physically able. The desert can and does kill with quiet, efficient ease.

Once you leave the blacktop you will use your four-wheel-drive capability only occasionally and usually in short spurts. The times will be few when you are constantly in four-wheel-drive. On the other hand, you will often find yourself enduring miles of bumpy, rocky road where the best thing your rig offers is durability rather than "double-traction" (which is what four-wheel-drive is called in Spanish).

Your rig will take a beating on these rough roads. Get out often and check the nuts and bolts to prevent them from rattling off. If some parts do rattle off, go back and look for them. More than one trip has been saved by finding a part lying back along the road.

Although the back roads of Baja may differ radically in terrain, from deep sand and cough-producing dust, to high mountains and riverbed granite, *they all share two common traits.*

First, in Baja, when you have averaged out time for photo stops, repairs, fast and slow parts of the trail, checking funny sounds, and admiring the view, you will always end up with a 10 mph average.

Second, to get somewhere the Mexican pickup driver has always had to follow the arroyos (riverbeds) and, when they end, the ridge tops. If the routes sometime seem whimsical it's because without a highway department you have to do a lot of winding around and going in and out of riverbeds to get from point A to point B in Baja.

Acquire a top rack with a positive attachment to the drip-rail. Do not use a pressure-mounted rubber-cushioned roof rack. They are made for the blacktop and will slowly disintegrate in offbeat Baja.

Carry your gas cans on exterior mounts. If you have a long rig you probably won't want to add the extra 100 pounds of weight over your rear bumper. However, in Baja, I never had any trouble with the 106-inch wheelbase of the 1970 FJ-55 Toyota Land-Cruiser I was driving.

Use of the winch is almost never required, but for peace of mind and the real safety it offers I would never go into Baja without one. As often happens, your winch will probably see use in assisting Mexican truckers. Be careful here: They get stuck because of their big loads or the occasional spots of really deep muck, so don't destroy your winch trying to make it do a job too big for it.

If you have your winch then take a snatch-block and good length of chain to double your pulling strength. Although trees or other objects to attach a winch to are rare in Baja it is better to have the equipment with you than back home in the garage. The old axiom, "If you are prepared for trouble you won't have it," is true in the mountains, deserts, beaches, and salt flats of Baja.

It is possible to go into Baja on stock tires, but oversized wheels and tires actually work better and provide an important measure of security and confidence, particularly where cactus spines are concerned. Plenty of them lie like nails hidden in the road, while the cholla cactus spreads its little windblown delights like cactus grenades all over Baja's dirt roads.

The big tires I had on the Toyota—Concorde Deserters, from Wheels West in Salinas—were punctured many times; at one point a sharp stick passed entirely through the outer tread, where it remained for several hundred miles. Yet in more than 5000 miles in two months in Baja on a recent trip I didn't have one flat. That alone is worth the big tires.

The big tires have another function. In sand the air pressure can be reduced to increase their flotation capacity. However, I recommend this maneuver only for emergencies, not as a regular practice: The trade-off danger of a tire coming off the rim is not worth it. When you have to reduce pressure, keep at least 10 pounds of air in the tires.

What to take? This is a tough question because it depends on why you are going to Baja and whether the trip is short or long. And one of the troubles with a four-wheel-drive vehicle is that there is room to take too much. At the end of this chapter I have listed some things that should be included in any offroad trip in Baja, whether long or short. Certainly it is possible to add or subtract from this list or to increase or decrease the amounts of supplies, since much will always depend on experience and goals. Camping preferences differ widely, and how much or little you haul with you will depend on what you want from the trip.

What about engine maintenance in the dirt and dust of Baja? Change the oil every thousand miles in Baja; the oil filter every 2000; and the air filter every three thousand—the last two every 1000 miles if you are in thick powdery dust for more than two or three days or more than 100 steady miles.

You can purchase oil of the viscosity you want in Baja, but probably not the exact brand you want. However, most American brands are available up and down Baja in varying quantities. If you carry one emergency change with you, you can buy what oil you need as you go; this will save weight and space in your rig. The cost of oil in Baja, even after devaluation, is about the same as in the States: near $1 American per quart.

Carry with you a set of metric or standard tools to meet the exact needs of your vehicle. And for changing oil an oversized "helper" for your drain-plug sockethead. Check your lug bolts often. It's a good excuse for a stretch. Carry a four-way lug wrench, the only tool able to reach the lugs on the big wheels and a good tool for loosening those annoying air-tightened lugs.

Mexican gasoline will not damage your plugs or engine. You may pick up some carbon and notice a "ping" from time to time, or get a case of preignition knock because of the low octane, but the real problem is getting lead for your engine (assuming it requires it), because Mexico's only decent gasoline, the high-octane Extra, is unleaded. The only source of lead is from low-octane Nova.

If your engine requires lead you may choose to run it on a half-and-half mixture of Extra and Nova. Most find this unsatisfactory, since 50% Nova brings on the pings and knocks, so the combination of 25% Nova and 75% Extra seems to be the most popular.

The speed limits are posted in kilometers. There is no Highway Patrol or State Trooper system. However, the Department of Tourism has divided Baja into rough 100-mile-long sections, each of which is patrolled daily by a bright green and white pickup equipped to perform emergency road service and give directions and assistance. They are called *The Green Angels* and usually one of the men in the two-man teams will know some English.

Mex 1 is generally a good road and well maintained, but it is without shoulders and its many *sharp* curves and steeply dropping grades can be very *tricky*. Please don't forget this. What a shame it would be to lose your rig on the blacktop before even getting it onto the desert and beaches.

Mexican trucks and buses ask no quarter and give none. As an American driver you are safest getting out of their way. They will pass you on hills, you will meet them coming uphill at you, and your only protection is to get out of the way. Be prepared in Baja to do some pretty fancy defensive driving.

Rear left blinker lights are used by Mexican truckers to signal those behind them, both day and night, that it is safe to pass them. Since this is of course the same signal used for a left turn, be careful before you respond to it. You will find it often given; and if you are going slowly uphill yourself, you are expected to give it, too.

With big, tough tires, you should have no flats in Baja, but if you do, and you can't get a jack under it, and are in a bad spot, use a Mexican jack: First put a rock under the axle to hold it right where it is; then dig a hole under your tire. Off comes the flat, on goes the spare; drive out of the hole. Nothing to it.

Keep a pair of long-nose pliers around. Among their many varied uses is getting cactus spines out from between the treads of your precious tires.

I do not recommend no-flat in four-wheel-drive oversized tires because if you do get a flat it makes patchwork messy, and because the chance of getting a flat on the big tires is small.

If you plan on bouncing for more than a day or two around the back roads, do get yourself a soft seat— but not driving gloves or one of those wheel-covers that provide a friction surface for a better grip. They're just a fine way to break your thumbs off when one of those big super-tires drops in a hole and spins the steering wheel around in a fast blur. Ouch!

This spin, incidentally, happens most often at creeping-slow speeds when you accidentally roll up against a big rock and put the full fulcrum weight of the auto against the steering gear to the steering wheel. Poise those hands far above the wheel; when it's all through start again.

Be prepared on the back roads for a constant film of dust. Unlike the bikers who can stay ahead of their dust, the four-wheel-driver has to be prepared to eat his. Anything valuable like cameras or fishing gear, must be packed well, and if you want to keep it free of dust, keep it packed. And of course what one writer described as "Gotcha Dust" will always be with you. Every time you slow or halt it will billow around you in clouds. Sometimes in Baja, in the limestone based areas, and in the rocks, and over some ridges, the dust is temporarily absent and the travel pleasant.

What about camping at night in Baja? It's easy and a money saver. You can halt virtually anywhere, put up a tent and sleep, arise the next morning and con-

tinue on. Naturally, some spots are quieter, more scenic, or safer than others, so pick the kind of place you want. And of course trying to camp near a city would be foolish for several reasons, disturbances by dogs and people foremost among them.

Another word of warning about camping on the back roads is one you wouldn't expect. These rough roads get a surprising amount of night travel by determined and busy Mexican rancheros, and it is their custom, whether in friendliness or good humor, to honk at every camp site they see. Moral: If you camp on a back road at night, camp out of sight.

As I said earlier, there is no need to fear banditos, particularly in offbeat Baja. Urban centers are where that problem is likely to occur, if it occurs at all. And when near an urban center it is wise to choose either a motel or commercial campground, many of which are in Baja, as detailed in Richard Carroll's accurate book *The Motor Camper's Guide to Mexico and Baja California.*

If you can, go to Baja with one or more companion vehicles. With joint supplies and experience each can lighten the load of the other, both mentally and physically. But if you cannot find someone to go with you, don't let that stop you from going. Just be sure to choose safer, less risky roads and goals, and move over them with the sobering knowledge that you are on your own.

Last but not least are some words of wisdom passed on to me by two Sierra and Baja four-wheel veterans, Dan Tolleson and Les Leslie: "Keep your foot off the clutch; drive *over* the rocks." They mean in compound, four-wheel-drive to let the engine have its head, just steer on idle. And in bad country don't try to drive around the big rocks coming in series. Drive over them. Your rig is built for it; your tires were meant for it. They can take it, but your transmission can't. In Baja in the rough spots it's foot off the clutch, tires up on the rocks.

The long peninsula holds for each its special pleasures and attractions, and certainly four-wheeling Baja does possess a sure guarantee of adventure, and that means every day: the crescent beach in the distance from the hard-won hill, the smell of ocean spray at Malarrimo from the final bend in the arroyo, the cry of sea birds when the engine is killed, and those endless starlit nights around the quiet, fireless camp. Oh that Baja. What a place.

The Four-Wheel-Drive Take-List

1. Good shovel.
2. Jumper cables.
3. Hydraulic jack and good solid wood base.
4. Handyman bumper jack and good solid wood base.
5. Two five-gallon gasoline cans (designed for gasoline only).
6. Two secure five-gallon water jugs (designed for water only).
7. One secure one-gallon water jug for daily use in motion.
8. Road flares.
9. Snatch block and stout 20-foot chain for block and tackle hookup.
10. Tire-changing irons and tire-patching kit.
11. Manual tire pump.
12. Spark-plug/tire-inflator unit.
13. Tire pressure gauge.
14. Four-way lug wrench.
15. Gasoline funnel that will fit in the neck of your gas tank (check before going).
16. Chamois cloth for filtering "country gasoline"
17. 10-foot length of garden hose or plastic squeeze pump for tank-to-tank transfer.
18. 50-feet ⅜" rope.
19. 50-feet nylon cord.
20. Large roll duc tape.
21. Two pair heavy-duty cotton gloves for winch-work and high-sierra cold.
22. Come-along.
23. Burlap sacks. (these are used empty to increase traction).
24. One set spark plugs.
25. New fan belt installed and carry one extra.
26. One oil filter (more for longer trip).
27. One air filter (more for longer trip).
28. Spare drain plugs (one for each plug).
29. Stove wire, electric wire, electric cord, and spare nuts & bolts.
30. Spare gas filter, either in-line or regular.
31. Fuses.
32. Spare *key* to vehicle.
33. Repair manual for your vehicle (*not* factory supplied booklet).
34. Complete tool kit including ratchet and sockets and box end wrenches.
35. One emergency change of oil.
36. Following Fluids: *brake, transmission, clutch, radiator coolant.* One pint each.
37. One can radiator sealer.
38. Extra-long ratchet handle for crackcase drain-plug socket.
39. Oil filter wrench.
40. Carpenter's hammer, 16 oz.
41. Small sledge hammer (for fender repair).
42. Hacksaw, sturdy.
43. Flashlight.
44. Whiskbroom for interior.
45. Dust cloths, several old towels preferable.
46. Window cleaner.
47. Paper towels.
48. Hand rags for changing oil and other mechanical work.
49. One can WD-40 lubricant.

THE CAMERA IN BAJA

by Robert Western

I reached for my camera and 600 mm lens. My hand came away gritty. The lens was so covered with dust the black finish was now a light tan. As I picked up the "600" the lens disconnected itself from the camera and bounced twice before coming to rest at my feet. I reconnected the camera to the lens and braced it on the window. Now it wouldn't focus. A glance at the front element found it covered with fine golden dust, which had worked its way past the lens cap. I pulled out my blower brush and rearranged the dust on the glass. After several frustrating moments the center of the lens seemed clean and I quickly refocused. The bird I was photographing in Baja's desert spun around on the cactus, exposed a featureless back, crouched for a moment, and flew off along the elephant trees and cholla cactus. I didn't get a picture.

Such can be the life of a photographer in Lower California. But despite the rather bleak picture I have painted thus far, there are only four environmental problems to consider while carrying a camera in Baja; dust, vibration, heat and static electricity. With only a slight investment in time and money, these problems can be licked, and you can return home with good pictures and undamaged equipment.

Dust: Baja dust has two aggravating properties, it is very fine and statically charged. This means it will get into totally unexpected places and stick with electromagnetic tenacity. Unfortunately the only foolproof method of preventing dust intrusion is to seal your camera in a plastic bag and leave it home. The situation is far from hopeless however, as long as you establish a daily routine of equipment maintenance.

About half the dust problem can be solved by keeping your equipment covered while on the move. For those who will be shooting only a few rolls on an entire trip, you should keep your camera in a bag or other enclosed area. For the habitual shooter of more than a roll per day, you will want your camera as accessible as possible. In this case the camera can be wrapped in a towel or shirt; making it available for those "once in a lifetime" shots and protecting it at the same time.

Fine clinging dust can be devastating to picture quality, so be sure your lens is clean before every shot. To prevent wear and tear on fine lens elements it is advisable to use protective filters, such as a Skylight or UV Haze. Reserve lens fluid and lens tissue for smudges, and remove the dust and grit with an anti-static brush before cleaning with a tissue. Anti-static brushes are more effective at removing charged dust particles than conventional camels hair brushes, and can be found in most camera stores and some record shops.

An almost indispensable tool is a can of compressed air. A number of brands are available in camera stores and usually come with some type of nozzle attachment for reaching otherwise inaccessible areas. I recommend using a brand that doesn't use freon as a propellant. Freon can escape with the air and leave greasy smudges on your lens. Always use short bursts of air to conserve your supply and concentrate your efforts around moving parts and lens mounts. Be extremely careful when using forced air on the inside of your camera. Never fire the air directly at shutter curtains or blades, as you might misalign or damage

---

Lighting emphasizes the unusual rock formations.

144

the mechanism. And pay special attention to the film pressure plate, as one piece of grit in this area can scratch an entire roll.

Vibration: Those of you who are familiar with four-wheeling off the pavement are probably aware of the subtle effects of vibrations. Mechanical and electrical devices can suffer unnoticed damage after being subjected to an afternoon of washboard or gravel riverbeds. Even the most rugged cameras must be carefully monitored against costly vibration damage. Each day you should check and retighten all screws on lenses and camera bodies. Carefully twist interchangeable lenses to be sure of a good solid mounting to the camera. If a lens can be moved even a fraction after it has been properly seated, then the mount/locking mechanism is either worn or loose from vibration.

The worst vibration problem is shock, caused by a small expensive piece of camera gear falling against a large immoveable object. This is a major problem on rutty roads where vehicles and contents can often be found hanging momentarily in midair after passing an unexpectedly bad bump. The car, being heavier than its contents, descends first, leaving passengers and equipment hanging alone for a split second before they too plummet earthward. The shocks on the car are designed to accept this kind of punishment, but not so your camera. Always carry pads of foam rubber or some similar material. Two inch thick pads are available in many lengths and make great pillows for the backside as well as equipment protectors.

For those whose equipment investment is extensive enough to justify aluminum camera cases, be sure that each piece of gear is separated from another by at least an inch of foam. In the absence of foam, crumpled newspaper or clothing makes good firm padding.

Heat: Baja weather is moderately seasonal. During the summer and early fall you may encounter temperatures over a hundred degrees, while in winter it ranges from balmy to comfortably hot in the afternoons and quite cool in the night and mornings.

Ruins of an adobe mission.

Altitude also plays a roll in climate, and you may be in 80° F. weather on the plains and find yourself in freezing snow in the high mountains.

A good rule to follow anywhere, is to never leave your camera in the hot sun, sitting on the dashboard, or in the glove compartment. These are all places where heat can rise way beyond the normal air temperature and damage the camera and film. Many modern cameras are made of plastic or have plastic parts. These have been known to melt during long exposure to excessive heat in a closed car. If you have gone to the precaution of wrapping your equipment in a shirt or similar object, against the hazards of vibration and dust, then it is fairly safe from heat damage, but the film may not be. Most films store well for up to two weeks or more at 75° F. or lower, but can be ruined by even a short exposure to higher temperatures.

A little trick I learned on my last trip on the Peninsula will come in handy for those who wish to keep their film and refreshments cool on a long day's trek. Carry a well insulated cooler (Styrofoam works wonders and is very light weight) for your film and drinks, and leave the lid off during the night. Since the nights are typically chilly in much of Baja, the film and other supplies will cool down nicely. Replace the lid firmly in the morning and everything will stay remarkably cold all day. One extra note of caution; if you place film and food together it is best to keep the film in a plastic bag, in case something spills.

Static Electricity: Static is a product of low humidity. Dry air is a Godsend if you are used to the water and salt-laden air of the coast, but it also encourages static discharges. This unseen problem has ruined many a promising photograph with tiny spider web-like tracks on the emulsion. The only practical solution is to advance and rewind the film slowly. If you notice your hair straying mysteriously from your head to nearby objects, or you get a mild shock when reaching for the door handle, then everything around you is carrying an electrical charge, and you should take extra care when handling your film.

Cameras and the Law: Apart from environmental problems you could have governmental problems while in Mexico. According to official Mexican law each person entering the country can have one still camera and/or movie camera and ten rolls of film. The average tourist probably will not shoot more than five rolls on an entire trip, but real photo enthusiasts may find themselves sorely restricted. There are two solutions to this dilemma, one is to bring what film you feel you need, beyond the limit, and risk having it taken away at any time you are in the country; and the other solution is to buy what film you need in Mexico. Either way can be quite costly. At present a 36 exposure roll of Kodachrome 64 slide film is selling for $5.00 American, and black & white film is virtually impossible to find at all. Laws such as these were designed to stop illegal traffic of foreign goods into Mexico. Usually they are not enforced on the tourist, but breaking any law in Mexico, no matter how minor, could mean confiscation of your equipment and tiresome delays.

Since the majority of today's cameras are of foreign manufacture, you could find yourself paying unnecessary duty when you return to the U.S. Customs before you enter Mexico. Contact your local customs office (listed under United States Government in the white pages of the phone directory) and make an appointment for an inspection of all camera equipment that has not been made in the United States. If you have only a few items to certify, the preprinted customs forms will be adequate; if you have lots of gear, then make your own list, with serial numbers and a short description of each item.

If your investment is great enough you should have extra insurance coverage. If you already have homeowners insurance the procedure is relatively simple. A separate rider can be put on your current policy, called All Risk/World Wide coverage. This means that no matter how your equipment suffers a loss and no matter where in the world you lost it, you are still covered, with no deductible. The rates for this type of coverage vary somewhat from company to company, but generally they are quite reasonable.

Camera Maintenance Equipment
1. Jeweler's screwdrivers.
2. Small hand towel.
3. Foam pad.
4. Lens tissue.
5. Lens cleaning fluid.
6. Compressed air with fine nozzle attachment.
7. Protective filters (Skylight, UV Haze, etc.).
8. Anti-static brush.

SELECTED BIBLIOGRAPHY
FOR FURTHER READING

Listed alphabetically by author the books named here represent various viewpoints and disciplines concerning both Baja California and the Mexican people. Some concern travel only, while others deal with cultural, historical, or philosophic problems pertinent both to Mexico and its two states: Baja California and Baja California Sur. Each book makes important contributions; some on how to travel there, others on how to better understand the people and their land.

Revolution! Mexico 1910–1920, Ronald Atkin. Macmillan, London, 1969.

The Flight of the Least Petrel, Griffing Bancroft. Putnam's, N.Y., 1932.

The Motor Camper's Guide to Mexico and Baja California, Richard Carroll. Chronicle Books, San Francisco, 1975.

A Field Guide to the Common and Interesting Plants of Baja California, Jeanette Coyle & Norman Roberts. Natural History Publishing Co., La Jolla, CA, 1976.

The Cave Paintings of Baja California, Harry Crosby, Copley Books, 1975.

Baja Handbook, James T. Crow. Cepek Co. Southgate, CA, 1974.

The People's Guide to Mexico, Carl Franz. Muir Press, Santa Fe, N.M., 1974.

A Land of Shorter Shadows, Erle Stanley Gardner. Wm. Morrow & Sons, N.Y., 1948.

Hunting the Desert Whale, ————, 1960.

Hovering over Baja, ————, 1961.

Off the Beaten Track in Baja, ————, 1967.

Mexico's Magic Square, ————, 1968.

The Hidden Heart of Baja, ————, 1962.

Lower California Guide, Gulick and Wheelock. A. H. Clark, Glendale, CA, 1975.

Baja California, Wm. Weber Johnson. Time-Life Books, N.Y., 1972.

Weed, Jerry Kamstra, Harper & Row, N.Y., 1974.

Baja California and the Geography of Hope, J. W. Krutch, Sierra Club, San Francisco, 1967.

The Forgotten Peninsula, J. W. Krutch. Wm. Morrow & Sons, N.Y., 1961.

The Children of Sanchez, Oscar Lewis, Penguin, Baltimore, MD, 1961.

A Death in the Sanchez Family, ————, 1969.

A History of Lower California, Pablo I. Martinez, Mexico City, 1961.

There It Is: Baja! Mike McMahan. Maneisser Press, Riverside, CA, 1972.

The Baja Book, Miller & Baxter. Baja Trails Pub., Santa Ana, CA, 1974.

Cruising the Sea of Cortez, Murray & Poole, Best-West Pub., Los Angeles, 1967.

Camp and Camino in Lower California, A. W. North. Baker & Taylor, N.Y., 1910.

Labyrinth of Solitude, Octavio Paz. Grove Press, N.Y., 1961

The Other Mexico, ————, 1972.

An Anthology of Mexican Poetry, Octavio Paz, ed. Indiana U. Press, Bloomington, 1971.

Baja California: Vanished Missions, Lost Treasures, Choral Pepper. Ward Ritchie Press, Pasadena, CA, 1975.

God and Mr. Gomez, Jack Smith. Reader's Digest Books, N.Y., 1974.

The Log of the Sea of Cortez, John Steinbeck. Viking Press, N.Y., 1941.

Map 1 **Baja California**

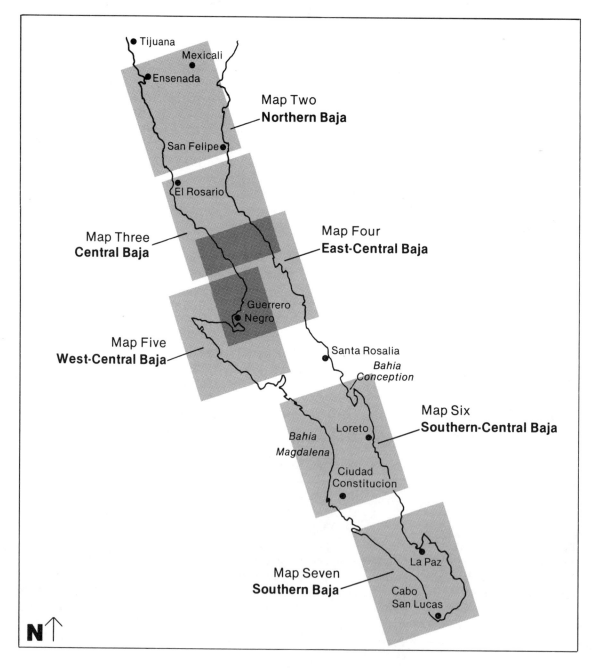

- Tijuana
- Mexicali
- Ensenada

Map Two
Northern Baja

- San Felipe
- El Rosario

Map Three
Central Baja

Map Four
East-Central Baja

- Guerrero Negro

Map Five
West-Central Baja

- Santa Rosalia
- *Bahia Conception*

Map Six
Southern-Central Baja

- Loreto
- *Bahia Magdalena*
- Ciudad Constitucion

- La Paz

Map Seven
Southern Baja

- Cabo San Lucas

N↑

Map 2 **Northern Baja**

MEX 1, 2, 5   BC 16
OFFBEAT ROAD LOGS

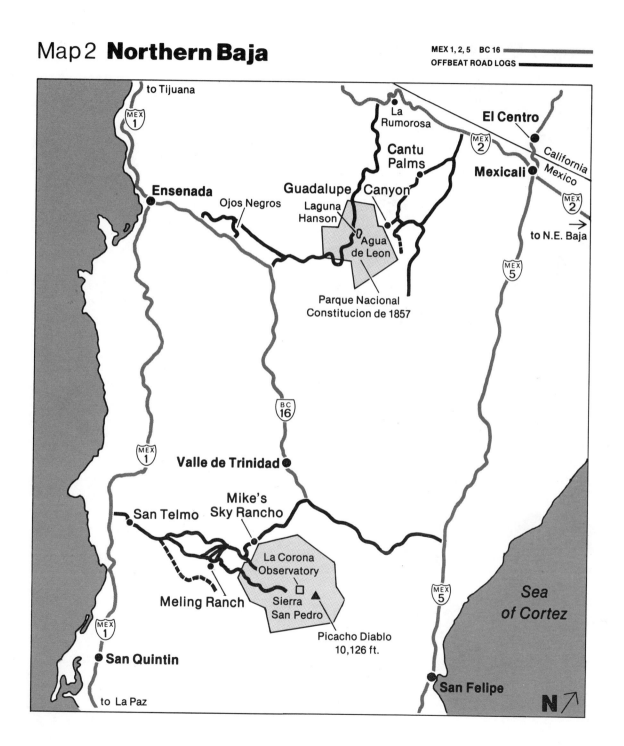

to Tijuana

MEX 1

La Rumorosa

El Centro

Cantu Palms

MEX 2

Mexicali

California
Mexico

Ensenada

Guadalupe Canyon

Ojos Negros

Laguna Hanson

MEX 2

to N.E. Baja

Agua de Leon

MEX 5

Parque Nacional
Constitucion de 1857

BC 16

MEX 1

Valle de Trinidad

Mike's Sky Rancho

San Telmo

La Corona Observatory

Meling Ranch

Sierra San Pedro

MEX 5

Sea of Cortez

MEX 1

Picacho Diablo
10,126 ft.

San Quintin

San Felipe

to La Paz

N

Map 3 **Central Baja**

MEX 1 ▬▬▬▬
OFFBEAT ROAD LOGS ▬▬▬▬

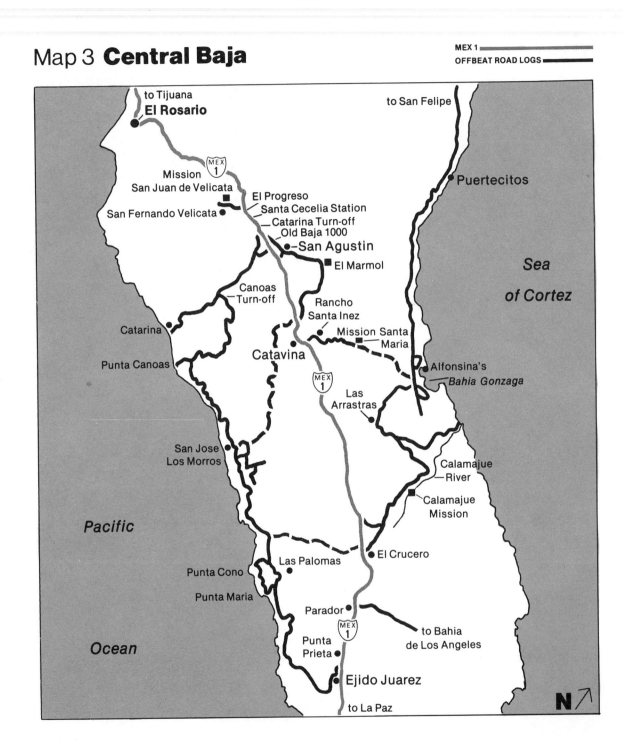

to Tijuana
El Rosario

to San Felipe

MEX 1

Mission
San Juan de Velicata

El Progreso
Santa Cecelia Station
Catarina Turn-off
Old Baja 1000

San Fernando Velicata

● Puertecitos

San Agustin

El Marmol

Sea
of Cortez

Canoas
Turn-off

Rancho
Santa Inez

Mission Santa
Maria

Catarina

Catavina

Punta Canoas

Alfonsina's
Bahia Gonzaga

MEX 1

Las
Arrastras

Pacific

San Jose
Los Morros

Calamajue
River

Calamajue
Mission

El Crucero

Las Palomas

Punta Cono

Punta Maria

Parador

MEX 1

Ocean

to Bahia
de Los Angeles

Punta
Prieta

● Ejido Juarez

to La Paz

N ↗

Map 4 **East-Central Baja**

MEX 1 ━━━━━━
OFFBEAT ROAD LOGS ━━━

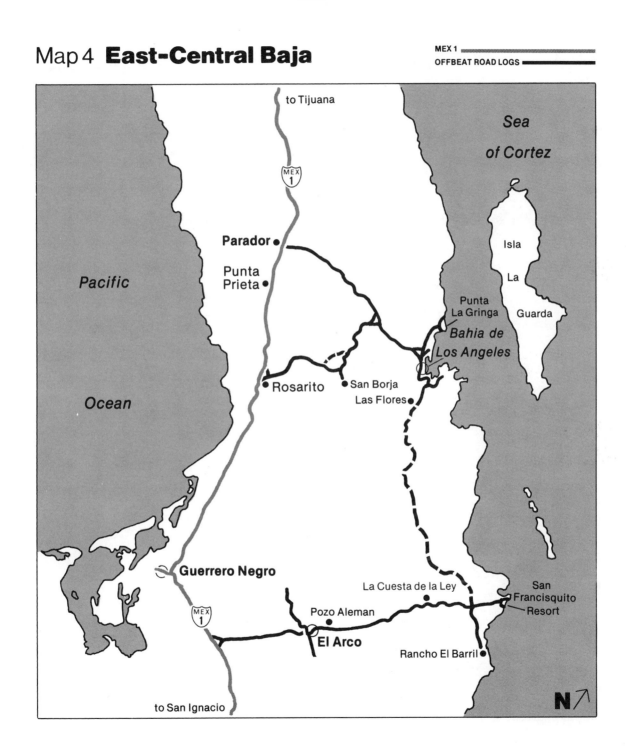

Map 5 **West-Central Baja**

MEX 1 ▬▬
OFFBEAT ROADS LOGS ▬▬

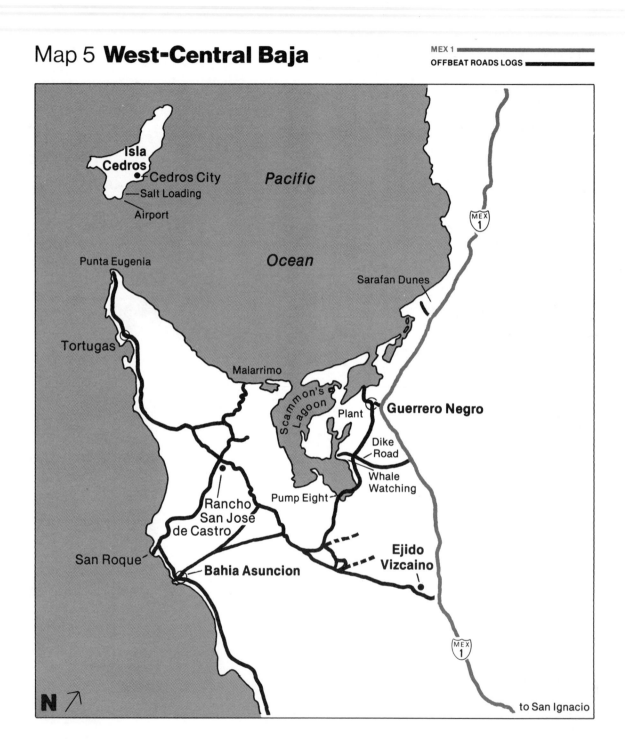

Isla Cedros
Cedros City
Salt Loading
Airport
Pacific
Punta Eugenia
Ocean
Sarafan Dunes
Tortugas
Malarrimo
Scammon's Lagoon
Plant
Guerrero Negro
MEX 1
Dike Road
Whale Watching
Pump Eight
Rancho San José de Castro
Ejido Vizcaino
San Roque
Bahia Asuncion
MEX 1
N
to San Ignacio

Map 6 **Southern-Central Baja**

MEX 1
OFFBEAT ROAD LOGS

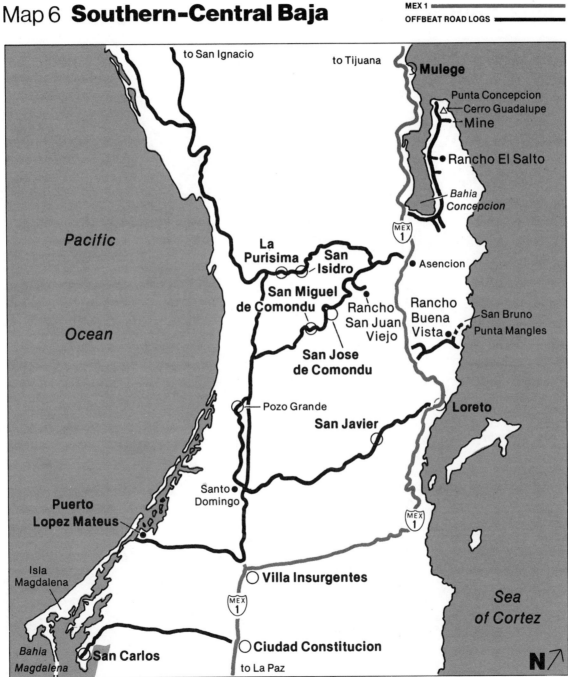

to San Ignacio

to Tijuana

Mulege

Punta Concepcion
Cerro Guadalupe
Mine

Rancho El Salto

Bahia Concepcion

MEX 1

Pacific

La Purisima

San Isidro

Asencion

San Miguel de Comondu

Rancho San Juan Viejo

Rancho Buena Vista

San Bruno
Punta Mangles

Ocean

San Jose de Comondu

Pozo Grande

Loreto

San Javier

MEX 1

Santo Domingo

Puerto Lopez Mateus

Isla Magdalena

Villa Insurgentes

MEX 1

Sea of Cortez

Bahia Magdalena

San Carlos

Ciudad Constitucion

to La Paz

N

Map 7 **Southern Baja**

MEX 1 ▬▬▬▬
OFFBEAT ROADS LOGS ▬▬▬▬

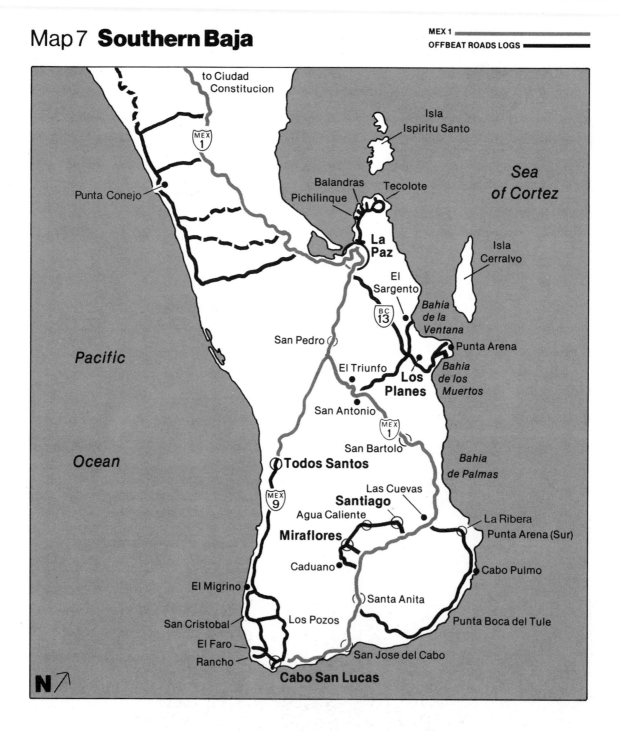